# VEGAN

## COOKBOOK

*365 DAYS OF QUICK & EASY PLANT-BASED RECIPES*
*FOR A CLEAN & HEALTHY DIET*

BY DEBBY HAYES

# TABLE OF CONTENTS

# INTRODUCTION

Not so long ago, people who didn't eat any animal products were thought to be a bit quirky. When they were invited to a dinner party, the host would make apologies for not knowing what to cook for them and simply give them the vegetables and potatoes that were meant as side dishes for the roast. If they were lucky, their well-meaning host would prepare a giant mushroom filled with cream cheese, or a stuffed red pepper for them, not understanding that cheese and bacon don't feature in a vegan diet.

All that has changed. The vegan diet has been given a boost in popularity, and plant-based diets have become trendy; it is something all the cool kids are doing. Some people have chosen to jump in with both feet, swearing off meat and all other animal products for good. Others have embraced "meat-free Mondays" as their contribution to the environment. Either way, human beings are starting to eat more plants.

Whether you are a longstanding, die-hard vegan, or you are just starting to experiment with some plant-based meals, learning how to create a tasty meal using only plants will make your journey more enjoyable. You will soon discover that the best dishes are the ones you have prepared from scratch, without using the highly processed meat alternatives that are found in the freezer section of the supermarket. Those are definitely useful to have on hand for days when you just don't feel like cooking, but your taste buds will be asking you what happened to the wonderful taste sensations you are able to create from whole foods.

Vegetables, whole grains, legumes, nuts, seeds, and healthy plant oils can be combined in an infinite number of ways. By adding herbs and spices, as well as aromatics, such as onions and garlic, you can create endless menu options. Gone are the days when stuffed mushrooms and peppers were the height of vegan fare.

The modern vegan diet includes mouthwatering chickpea curries, black bean burgers, spicy lentil soups, inspired tofu dishes, and colorful power bowls. Even the most hardened meat lovers have to admit that they don't miss the meat when a little creativity is used to prepare a hearty, meat-free meal.

I have to admit that I really enjoy challenging my guests with a vegan meal from time to time. My family have grown to look forward to the more interesting vegan meals I prepare for them. I keep the flavors interesting and the textures varied, and they usually don't miss the meat. In fact, more often than not, they ask for more! The recipes in this book will help you make both quick daily meals for the family and dinner party-worthy menus that will have everyone asking for the recipe.

# BURGEONING POPULARITY OF THE PLANT-BASED DIET

If you are jumping on the vegan bandwagon, you will, no doubt, have your reasons. You may have heard that it is good for the environment, or you may have been told that it is a healthy way of living. Maybe you are just curious or like to follow the trends. No matter what has driven you to leave out the animal products in your diet, you still need to enjoy what you are eating if you want it to become a way of life.

The modern vegan diet has grown in popularity in recent years, because there are so many more people who are interested in going plant-based than ever before. It is no longer a diet reserved for people who are considered a little quirky and difficult. The concept has been embraced by men, women, and children from all walks of life.

Gone are the days when your vegan friends were always the pale waifs with their heads in the clouds. With the growing popularity of this way of life, there is now a greater awareness about how to make sure you are healthy when excluding animal products from your diet. A vegan diet that includes foods from all food groups offers the same benefits as a well-balanced diet that includes meat.

Vegan diets of the past typically included a lot of vegetables, some boring beans, and snacks of nuts and seeds. Now that there are more and more people experimenting with plant-based eating, there is a greater variety of recipes available to anyone who wants to give it a try. Even if you don't know where to start, there are resources available to guide you on your path to a meat-free life, including this recipe book.

Grocery stores have also joined the revolution. With the growing demand for vegan products, you can now find many wonderful options in almost all stores. Plant-based products are taking up valuable retail space in order to meet the needs of people who care about their own health, as well as the wellbeing of the environment.

## THE PART-TIME VEGAN

In case you are feeling like you are in the wrong place, you don't have to be a card-carrying member of the vegan society to enjoy vegan food. Even the biggest meat-eater can, and in my opinion, should, enjoy a meat-free meal from time to time. Everyone can benefit from eating more plants.

If you do it right, and make sure your vegan meals are full of color, flavor, and texture, you won't feel hard done by when you skip the meat. Page through our recipes to find one that appeals to you most. If you enjoy your plant-based foods, you are more likely to come back for more.

Being a part-time vegan means that you increase your intake of plant-based foods, which has many benefits for your health, and for the environment. Plants are excellent sources of vital nutrition for human beings. A lot of the nutrients in the foods we eat in the modern world have been lost through processing, storing, and cooking practices. When you eat more vegetables, legumes, whole grains, nuts, and seeds, you are giving your health a boost with more fiber, vitamins, minerals, and phytonutrients.

## MEAT-FREE NUTRITIONAL BALANCE

Becoming vegan doesn't automatically guarantee good health. As is the case with conventional eating patterns, you still need to make sure to eat a variety of foods. The balance between food groups remains important in order for you to benefit from a plant-based diet. Becoming vegan does not simply mean leaving the meat off your plate. The nutrients you are losing when you quit animal products need to be replaced from other food sources.

A healthy plant-based diet includes foods from all of the food groups. It is amazing what nature provides for us in the form of plant foods. Fruits, vegetables, whole grains, legumes, nuts, and seeds, provide the human body with the full spectrum of nutrition.

A quick note on iron and vitamin B12:

- While plants do contain iron in the form of non-haem iron, it is not as well absorbed and used in the body as the haem iron we get from animal sources. Making sure to eat iron-rich foods, such as spinach and kale, with vitamin C-rich foods to enhance the absorption, goes a long way towards ensuring that you consume adequate amounts of plant-based iron. It is a good idea to keep an eye on your iron levels when choosing a plant-based diet.

- The best sources of vitamin B12 are animal proteins, such as red meat, fish, cheese, and eggs. It is also found in nutritional yeast and fortified cereals. If you are a full-time vegan, it may be a good idea to take a vitamin B12 supplement to make sure your body is getting enough of this important nutrient.

## GO VEGAN WITH A VARIETY OF VEGETABLES

Vegetables are the mainstay of a vegan diet. Your mother may have had to nag you to eat your veggies when you were a child, but she was on to something. Vegetables are where we get most of our nutrition. They offer vitamins, minerals, fiber, phytonutrients, and a little energy to keep our bodies functioning optimally.

No matter whether you are a meat eater or a vegan, vegetables should take up space on your plate. Ideally, they should form at least half of your meal. Not only are they good for you, but they bring a wonderful array of color to your plate, making your meals much more visually appealing. Red peppers, carrots, gem squash, broccoli, blue potatoes (yes, they exist), purple cabbage, and beetroot, make a rainbow of colors that meet your nutritional requirements.

With a little bit of creativity, your vegetables can take center stage on your plate. When meat is not the hero of your meal, vegetables are given a chance to shine. Instead of planning your meals around meat, fish, or chicken, now you are planning your meals so that roasted cauliflower steaks, giant mushrooms, and strips of butternut squash become exciting, flavorsome alternatives.

Vegetables are not just for steaming and serving alongside something that you really want to eat. They can and should be a feature of a meal. Make the most of their color, texture, and variety of flavors to make your meal mouth-wateringly delicious.

## USE GRAINS TO YOUR ADVANTAGE

Grains are an important component of the vegan diet. Not only do they provide you with energy in the form of carbohydrates, but they complement the protein from vegan protein sources, such as beans. In addition to that, they are excellent sources of both soluble and insoluble fiber, as well as important vitamins and minerals.

Grains can be the hero of your vegan meal, or a side dish that helps carry the flavor of your vegetables and sauces. Rice, quinoa, barley, and bulgar wheat add their own unique taste and texture to a meal. They offer an earthiness, or a nuttiness, or a sweetness, or a bitterness to your meals, creating balance in every mouthful.

To get the most out of your grains, opt for those that are only minimally processed. The brown options are always going to be better for you. They contain more fiber, and if the germ is intact, you will benefit from the healthy oils, proteins, and vitamins and minerals it contains.

# VEGAN PROTEIN POWER

Protein provides the amino acids our bodies need to build protein structures, such as muscles, antibodies, and enzymes. Without sufficient protein in our diets, our bodies would not be strong and healthy. That is why it is important to ensure an adequate protein intake when eating a vegan diet. Simply leaving meat off the plate, without replacing it with another protein source, will result in a protein deficiency.

If you are making the transition from animal proteins being your primary source of protein to plants being your only source of protein, it can be difficult to wrap your head around which foods to include in your diet. But once you get the hang of it, it becomes just as easy as popping a chicken fillet under the grill.

Beans, lentils, chickpeas, nuts, and seeds all contain significant amounts of protein. When you eat a variety of plant-based protein foods combined with grains and vegetables, you are able to provide your body with the full spectrum of amino acids it needs.

It can be extremely time consuming to rinse, soak, and then cook your beans and chickpeas, but if you prefer everything to be as fresh and wholesome as possible, then this is your best option. A handy hint when it comes to cooking your pulses from scratch is to cook them in your slow cooker. When you have some time, cook the whole bag, and then freeze the legumes in portions, ready for you to pop into your favorite recipe.

If long, slow cooking is not for you, then the canned options are just as good. They can be added to vegan curries, soups and stews, blitzed to make plant-based burgers, mashed to make a protein spread for bread, tossed into a salad, or pureed to make a healthy dip for vegetables. Nothing beats the versatility of legumes.

Foods made from soya beans, such as tofu and its fermented cousin, tempeh, are great sources of protein, and wonderful flavor carriers. Tofu is made by coagulating soy milk and pressing the liquid out of it to make tofu of varying textures, from soft to hard. It can be used in a wide variety of ways, making your vegan meals even more interesting.

# HEALTHY FATS FOR A HEALTHY VEGAN

A vegan diet is naturally low in saturated fats – the type of fat that has been linked to raised blood cholesterol levels and cardiovascular disease. Most saturated fat is found in animal products, and includes the fat on meat, the skin on chicken, cream, butter, and full fat dairy products. Since these foods don't form part of a vegan diet, it is easier for someone who chooses a vegan diet to control how much they eat.

The fat in a vegan diet is mostly in the form of unsaturated fats which provide the body with essential fatty acids that contribute to health, rather than promote disease. Avocados, nuts, seeds, olives, and oils, such as olive oil, provide us with healthy omega-3 fats that help to control chronic inflammation in the body.

# YOU DON'T NEED TO SKIP THE MILK: DAIRY ALTERNATIVES

The shelves in a modern grocery store contain a variety of dairy milk alternatives. You can buy soya milk, oat milk, rice milk, coconut milk, almond milk, or macadamia milk. You don't have to forego the milk in your coffee, or the creamy sauces you enjoy in your pasta. The best part is, you can now also find non-dairy yogurt and cheese options.

Each type of milk alternative comes with its own flavor profile. Everyone has their favorite. Some plant-based milks have a sweet taste that is great when used in hot beverages and baking, while others have a more savory flavor profile which works well in cooked dishes.

## Vegan Staples Shopping List

| Vegetables: | Fruits: | Grains: |
|---|---|---|
| Artichokes | Apple | Amaranth |
| Asparagus | Apricot | Barley |
| Beetroot | Banana | Buckwheat |
| Bok choy | Blackberries | Bulgar |
| Broccoli | Blueberries | Corn |
| Brussels sprouts | Cherries | Faro |
| Butternut squash | Coconut | Freekeh |
| Cabbage | Cranberries | Millet |
| Carrot | Dates | Oats |
| Cauliflower | Dragon fruit | Quinoa |
| Celery | Figs | Rice |
| Chard | Goji berries | Rye |
| Collard greens | Gooseberries | Sorghum |
| Cucumber | Grapes | Spelt |
| Eggplant | Grapefruit | Teff |
| Endive | Guava | Wheat |
| Fennel | Kiwifruit | Wild rice |
| Garlic | Kumquat | |
| Gem squash | Lemon | |
| Hubbard squash | Lime | |
| Jerusalem artichoke | Loquat | |
| Kale | Lychee | |
| Leek | Mango | |
| Lettuce | Melons | |
| Mushrooms | Mulberries | |
| Okra | Nectarine | |
| Onions | Orange | |
| Parsnips | Papaya | |
| Peppers – all colors | Passionfruit | |
| Potato | Paw-paw | |
| Radishes | Peach | |

| Vegetables: | Fruits: | Proteins: | |
|---|---|---|---|
| Rhubarb | Pear | Beans - adzuki, black fava, kidney, lima, pinto, soybeans | Seitan |
| Spinach | Plum | | Spelt |
| Spring onions | Pineapple | Chickpeas | Teff |
| Sweet corn | Pomegranate | Edamame | Tempeh |
| Sweet potato | Raspberries | Lentils | Tofu |
| Tomato | Strawberries | Nutritional yeast | |
| Turnip | Watermelon | | |
| Zucchini | | | |

| Healthy fats: | Dairy alternatives: | Flavor enhancers: | |
|---|---|---|---|
| Avocados | Almond milk | Capers | **Spices:** |
| Olives | Coconut milk | Chilis | Allspice |
| | Macadamia milk | Curry paste | Cardamom |
| **Oils:** | Oat milk | Dried mushrooms | Cayenne pepper |
| Almond oil | Rice milk | | Cinnamon |
| Canola oil | Soya milk | **Herbs:** | Cumin |
| Coconut oil | Vegan yogurt | Basil | Coriander |
| Macadamia nut oil | Vegan cheese | Bay leaves | Ginger |
| Olive oil | | Chives | Mustard |
| Peanut oil | | oriander | Paprika |
| | | Dill | Pepper |
| **Nuts:** | | Fennel | Nutmeg |
| Almonds | | Lemongrass | Turmeric |
| Brazil nuts | | Marjoram | |
| Cashews | | Mint | |
| Hazelnuts | | Oregano | Vinegar |
| Peanuts | | Parsley | Tomato paste |
| Pecan nuts | | Rosemary | |
| Pistachios | | Sage | |
| Walnuts | | Tarragon | |
| | | Thyme | |
| **Seeds:** | | | |
| Chia | | Lemon juice | |
| Flaxseeds | | Vegan Miso | |
| Hemp | | Nutritional yeast | |
| Pumpkin | | Vegan Soy sauce | |
| Sesame | | | |
| Sunflower | | | |

# ANIMAL INGREDIENTS THAT MIGHT BE HIDING IN YOUR FOOD

The last thing you want is to undo your vegan diet by not being aware of the less obvious animal ingredients that may be lurking in your seemingly plant-based food purchase. If you want to eat a strict plant-based diet without having to prepare all of your food from scratch, you will need to become an expert at reading food labels. Non-vegan ingredients that are commonly used in food products include:

- Albumin
- Aspic
- Casein
- Collagen
- Elastin
- Gelatin
- Keratin
- Lactose
- Lard
- Pepsin
- Carmine or cochineal - Red Dye 40
- Royal jelly
- Shellac
- Whey

# HEALTHY, TASTY, PLANT-BASED RECIPES

Eating a healthful, balanced, vegan diet is easy when you know how, and when you have the most amazing recipes at your fingertips. Our collection of recipes includes something for every palate. These recipes are simple to follow, and will help you ensure that you are meeting all of your nutritional requirements entirely from plants.

Whether you are following a vegan diet for your own health or for the wellbeing of the planet, you need to enjoy what you are eating if it is to become a sustainable way of life for you. Creating meals that include a variety of colorful vegetables, some earthy grains, and some plant-based protein, along with a dose of healthy fats and loads of flavor-enhancing ingredients, will have you asking for more.

Use this collection of recipes for your daily family meals. You can also wow your guests with a plate full of plants that will have them wondering why they are still making meat the hero of their meals. Plant-based ingredients come together to bring you a combination of fresh, wholesome flavors, a variety of interesting textures, and a riot of enticing colors that everyone will enjoy.

The benefits of a vegan diet are now well-recognized by many. There are still people who will tell you that they could not survive without meat, but you are no longer sitting on the sidelines if you have chosen to follow a plant-based diet. Your friends and family likely have a much greater awareness of your way of eating, and you are now much less likely to be given a plate of boring vegetables and rice or a stuffed mushroom when you are a guest at the dinner table. And if they haven't caught on just yet, why not recommend this vegan recipe book to open their eyes to a whole new world of tasty food.

# 28 Day Meal Plan

*B.* Breakfast    *L.* Lunch    *D.* Dinner

| DAY 1 | DAY 2 | DAY 3 | DAY 4 | DAY 5 |
|---|---|---|---|---|
| *B.* Simple Vegan Pancakes<br>*L.* Hearty Miso Mushroom Patties<br>*D.* Creamy Herb & Cauliflower Pasta | *B.* Avo & Salsa Tempeh Burritos<br>*L.* Crispy Grilled Eggplant & Soba Noodles<br>*D.* Madeira-glazed Sheppard's Pie | *B.* Cinnamon & Chocolate Banana Bread<br>*L.* Faux Meatballs<br>*D.* Sweet & Tangy Thai Fried Rice | *B.* Spicy Breakfast Chilaquiles<br>*L.* Russian-Dressed Reuben Burgers<br>*D.* Vegan Chili With A Twist | *B.* Versatile Oven-Baked Pancakes<br>*L.* Spicy Thai-Inspired Pumpkin Stew<br>*D.* Zesty Citrus Seitan |

| DAY 6 | DAY 7 | DAY 8 | DAY 9 | DAY 10 |
|---|---|---|---|---|
| *B.* Breakfast Bagel Sandwiches<br>*L.* Vegan-Style Tofu Pad Thai<br>*D.* Hearty Mushroom & Wine Polenta | *B.* Spring Onion & Edamame Rice Bowl<br>*L.* Tahini-Dressed Smoky Chickpea Wraps<br>*D.* Soupy Mushroom & Corn Chowder | *B.* Fiery Vegan Breakfast Tacos<br>*L.* Sweet & Savory Char Kway Teow<br>*D.* Smoky Yams & Black-Eyed Peas | *B.* Quick & Easy Breakfast Squares<br>*L.* Super Saucy Garlic Ziti<br>*D.* Spicy Chickpea Tikka Masala | *B.* Strawberry Cornmeal Waffles<br>*L.* Sweet & Smoky Tofu Sandwiches<br>*D.* Ginger & Garlic Broccoli Stir-Fry |

| DAY 11 | DAY 12 | DAY 13 | DAY 14 | DAY 15 |
|---|---|---|---|---|
| *B.* One-Pan Crispy Veg Bake<br>*L.* Sweet & Sticky BBQ Wraps<br>*D.* Vegan-Style Pepperoncini Pizza | *B.* Coconutty Chia Pudding<br>*L.* Sweet & Tangy Bahn Mi<br>*D.* Zesty Popping Pepper Cauliflower Wings! | *B.* Spicy Breakfast Chilaquiles<br>*L.* Nutty Smoked Chickpea Salad Sandwiches<br>*D.* Braised Imposter Pork | *B.* Best Banana Pancakes<br>*L.* Decadent Broccoli Farfalle Patsa<br>*D.* Comfy & Cozy Cauliflower Curry | *B.* Yam & Tofu Hash<br>*L.* Korean Veggie Bowls with Jackfruit<br>*D.* Decadent & Lush Mushroom Bolognese |

| DAY 16 | DAY 17 | DAY 18 | DAY 19 | DAY 20 |
|---|---|---|---|---|
| *B.* Autumn-Spiced Oatmeal Bread<br>*L.* Smoked Carrot & Tofu Rolls<br>*D.* Robust Chickpea & Noodle Soup | *B.* Very-Berry Vanilla Pancakes<br>*L.* Fresh Herb Tabbouleh<br>*D.* Spicy Pan-Seared Tempeh Steaks | *B.* Avo & Salsa Tempeh Burritos<br>*L.* Vegan San Choy Bow<br>*D.* Quick & Easy Pasta Fagioli | *B.* Versatile Oven-Baked Pancakes<br>*L.* Garden-Tossed Chickpea Salad<br>*D.* Spicy Mushroom Tetrazzini | *B.* Simple Vegan Pancakes<br>*L.* Creamy Vegan Mediterranean Burger<br>*D.* Old-School Southwestern Soup |

| DAY 21 | DAY 22 | DAY 23 | DAY 24 | DAY 25 |
|---|---|---|---|---|
| *B.* Cinnamon & Chocolate Banana Bread<br>*L.* Decadent Broccoli Farfalle Patsa<br>*D.* Vegan-Style Oven Stir-Fry | *B.* Strawberry Cornmeal Waffles<br>*L.* Hearty Mushroom & Brussels Wraps<br>*D.* Creamy Herb & Cauliflower Pasta | *B.* Breakfast Bagel Sandwiches<br>*L.* Crunchy Veg & Vermicelli Salad<br>*D.* Peppers & Zucchini Basil Pasta | *B.* Fiery Vegan Breakfast Tacos<br>*L.* Fan Favorite Broccoli Burritos<br>*D.* Hearty Mushroom & Wine Polenta | *B.* One-Pan Crispy Veg Bake<br>*L.* Nutty Philipines-Style Cashew Pasta<br>*D.* Spicy Yam & Squash Enchiladas |

| DAY 26 | DAY 27 | DAY 28 |
|---|---|---|
| *B.* Quick & Easy Breakfast Squares<br>*L.* Red Lentil & Navy Bean Patties<br>*D.* Peppers & Zucchini Basil Pasta | *B.* Yam & Tofu Hash<br>*L.* Beety-Roasted Quinoa Salad<br>*D.* Triple Threat Indonesian Fried-Rice | *B.* Spicy Breakfast Chilaquiles<br>*L.* Flavor-Filled Portobello Burgers<br>*D.* Vegan-Style Thai Green Curry |

# BREAKFASTS

# BEST BANANA PANCAKES

COOK TIME: 48 MINS | MAKES: 12 SERVINGS

## INGREDIENTS:

- 1/2 tsp. kosher salt
- 2 tsp. baking soda
- 2 tbsp. organic dark brown sugar
- 2 1/2 cups all-purpose flour
- 1 small mashed banana
- 2 cups soy milk
- Coconut oil for frying

## DIRECTIONS:

1. In a large bowl, sieve together the salt, baking soda, sugar, and flour. Whisk until the ingredients are properly combined. Create a well in the center of the flour mixture, and add the mashed banana and soy milk. Use a wooden spoon to gently mix all of the ingredients until just combined – you do not want to overmix the batter.

2. Heat a small amount of coconut oil in a large frying pan over medium heat. You only need enough coconut oil to grease the pan per pancake, if necessary. When the oil is nice and hot, pour about 1/3 cup of the batter into the hot pan. Fry for 2 minutes, or just until tiny bubbles appear on the surface of the pancake. Flip the pancake, and fry for an additional 1-2 minutes.

3. Transfer the cooked pancake to a plate, and keep warm while you repeat the process with the remaining batter, adding additional coconut oil between pancakes, as necessary.

4. Serve the pancakes warm with maple syrup and fruit, if desired.

# QUICK & EASY BREAKFAST SQUARES

COOK TIME: 25-30 MINS | MAKES: 10 SERVINGS

## INGREDIENTS:

- 1/4 cup raw millet
- 1/3 cup raw quinoa
- 2 cups raw rolled oats
- 1/2 cup dried apricots, chopped
- 1 cup mixed nuts, chopped
- 1/4 cup mixed seeds
- 1/4 tsp. kosher salt
- 1 tsp. pure vanilla essence
- 2 tbsp. organic dark brown sugar
- 1/4 cup pure coconut oil
- 1/2 cup almond butter
- 1/2 cup pure maple syrup

## DIRECTIONS:

1. Set the oven to preheat to 350°F, with the wire rack in the center of the oven. Line a large, square baking dish with greaseproof paper, leaving a bit of the paper to hang over the edges for handles.

2. Place a large frying pan over medium-low heat, and when the pan is nice and hot, dry roast the millet, quinoa, and rolled oats for about 3 minutes, or until nicely toasted. Meanwhile, stir together the apricots, nuts, and seeds in a large mixing bowl. Scrape the ingredients of the pan into the bowl of fruit, nuts, and seeds, add the salt, and stir to combine. Set aside.

3. In a small pot, stir together the vanilla essence, brown sugar, coconut oil, almond butter, and maple syrup. Place the pot over medium heat, and stir until all the ingredients are melted and nicely combined. Scrape the mixture into the bowl of fruit, nuts, seeds, and grains, and stir until everything is properly coated.

4. Scrape the mixture into the prepared baking dish, and use a wooden spoon or the bottom of a clean glass to press the mixture firmly into the dish in an even layer.

5. Bake in the oven for 25-30 minutes, or until the top is golden brown. Allow the dish to cool on the counter for a few minutes before refrigerating until cold. Once it is cold, use the edges of the greaseproof paper to lift the uncut square from the dish. Slice into 10 squares, and serve.

**Quick Tip:**
Any leftovers should be refrigerated in an airtight container for no more than 7 days.

# SIMPLE VEGAN PANCAKES

COOK TIME: 20-40 MINS | MAKES: 14 PANCAKES

## INGREDIENTS:

- 1 1/4 tsp. Himalayan salt
- 1/2 tsp. baking soda
- 4 tsp. baking powder
- 2 cups all-purpose flour, spooned and leveled
- 1 1/2 cups plus 2 tbsp. almond milk
- 2 tsp. vanilla essence
- 2 tsp. white vinegar
- 2 tbsp. pure maple syrup (plus more for serving)
- Coconut oil for frying

## DIRECTIONS:

1. Place the salt, baking soda, baking powder, and all-purpose flour in a medium-sized bowl, and whisk until properly combined.

2. In a separate mixing bowl, stir together the almond milk, vanilla, vinegar, and 2 tablespoons of maple syrup. Pour the mixture into the bowl of flour, and stir until you have a lump-free batter.

3. Place a large frying pan over medium-low heat, and when the pan is nice and hot, melt 1-2 teaspoons of coconut oil. You just need enough to coat the bottom of the pan.

4. When the oil has melted, add 1/4 cup of the batter to the pan. You may do more than 1 pancake at a time, as long as they are not touching. The pancakes should be at least 2 inches apart. Fry each pancake for 1-2 minutes, and flip when tiny bubbles appear on the surface. Fry the other side for an additional 1-2 minutes, or until both sides of each pancake are nicely browned. Transfer the cooked pancakes to a plate, and keep warm.

5. Repeat the process with the remaining batter, adding a little oil to the pan as needed between batches.

6. Serve the pancakes with additional warmed maple syrup if desired.

# YAM & TOFU HASH

COOK TIME: 30 MINS | MAKES: 4 SERVINGS

## INGREDIENTS:

- 8 oz. beets, peeled and cubed (1/2-inch cubes)
- 8 oz. yams, peeled and cubed (1/2-inch cubes)
- 8 oz. russet potatoes, peeled and cubed (1/2-inch cubes)
- Kosher salt
- White pepper
- 1/4 cup extra-virgin olive oil
- 8 oz. tofu, cubed (1/2-inch cubes)
- 1 tbsp. kikkoman soy sauce
- 1 shallot, finely chopped
- 1/2 tsp. fresh thyme leaves, minced
- 2 tsp. crushed garlic
- 1/3 cup coconut creamer
- 2 spring onions, thinly sliced (for garnish)

## DIRECTIONS:

1. In a large mixing bowl, toss together the beets, yams, and russet potatoes. Add 1/2 teaspoon each of salt and pepper, along with 1 tablespoon of olive oil. Toss until all of the ingredients are evenly coated. Cover the bowl and microwave for 8-10 minutes, or until the vegetables are fork-tender and the potatoes are no longer opaque around the edges.

2. In a large frying pan over medium-high heat, heat 1 tablespoon of olive oil. When the oil is nice and hot, add the tofu, soy sauce, and 1/4 teaspoon each of salt and pepper. Stir fry the tofu for 4-6 minutes, flipping at regular intervals until all the edges are nicely browned. Scrape the cooked tofu into a bowl, and keep warm.

3. In the same pan, heat the remaining 2 tablespoons of oil. When the oil is nice and hot, fry the shallots for 5 minutes until translucent. Add the thyme and crushed garlic, frying for 3o seconds while allowing the flavors to meld.

4. Add the microwaved vegetables to the pan with their juices, and stir in the coconut creamer. Spread the vegetables out over the pan, and press them down using the back of a spatula. Cook the hash for 6-8 minutes, or until it is evenly browned, carefully flipping the vegetables in sections every 2 minutes. Do not stir the pan while the vegetables cook.

5. Divide the cooked hash between 4 plates, and top with cooked tofu and spring onions before serving.

# ONE-PAN CRISPY VEG BAKE

COOK TIME: 30 MINS | MAKES: 4 SERVINGS

## INGREDIENTS:

- 4 cups frozen hash browns, shredded
- Cooking spray
- 1/2 tsp. old bay seasoning
- 1 1/2 tsp. kosher salt (divided)
- 1/2 tsp. freshly ground black pepper
- 14 oz. extra-firm tofu, drained and crumbled
- 1/2 tsp. Himalayan black salt
- 1/2 tsp. ground turmeric
- 1/4 cup nutritional yeast
- 1 cup button mushrooms, sliced
- 1/2 red onion, thinly sliced
- 1 red bell pepper, roughly chopped
- 2 cups kale, chopped
- 4 spring onions, thinly sliced (for garnish)

## DIRECTIONS:

1. Set the oven to preheat to 415°F, with the wire rack in the center of the oven. Line a large baking sheet with greaseproof paper.

2. Spread the shredded hash browns out in a single layer on the prepared baking sheet. Coat with cooking spray, and season with old bay seasoning, 1 teaspoon of salt, and pepper. Toss until everything is evenly coated in the spices. Bake in the oven for 10 minutes.

3. In a medium-sized mixing bowl, toss the tofu with the remaining kosher salt, Himalayan black salt, turmeric, and nutritional yeast. Remove the sheet from the oven, and flip the potatoes with a spatula before shifting them to the side. Spray the sheet with cooking spray, and add the seasoned tofu to the center of the sheet. Add the mushrooms, onions, and bell pepper to the other end of the pan, and spray everything with a final layer of cooking spray.

4. Place the sheet back in the oven for 20 minutes, and flip everything half way through. The potatoes should darken, the tofu should become crisp around the edges, and the vegetables should be fork-tender.

5. Transfer the sheet to a wooden chopping board, and immediately place the kale over everything. Toss the kale through the cooked food for a few minutes, or until just wilted.

6. Once the kale is mixed all the way through, spoon the contents of the sheet into 4 bowls, and sprinkle with spring onions before serving.

# AVO & SALSA TEMPEH BURRITOS

COOK TIME: 10-15 MINS | MAKES: 4 SERVINGS

## INGREDIENTS:

- 1 tbsp. extra-virgin olive oil
- 14 oz. firm tempeh, rinsed and patted dry
- 1/2 cup store-bought salsa
- 4 large flour tortillas
- 16 cherry tomatoes, quartered
- 1 Hass avocado, sliced
- Himalayan salt
- Freshly ground black pepper
- Fresh coriander leaves, chopped (for serving)
- Sriracha sauce

## DIRECTIONS:

1. Heat the oil in a medium frying pan over medium-high heat. When the oil is nice and hot, break the tempeh up into small pieces and fry for 2-3 minutes, or until any water has evaporated and the tempeh is hot. Add the salsa, and stir for 1-2 minutes until warmed.

2. Heat the tortillas in a dry frying pan over medium-high heat, until each side is lightly toasted. Alternatively, you may drag the tortillas directly over a burner flame for a few seconds at a time with metal tongs, until the tortillas are nicely toasted.

3. Build your burritos by dividing the contents of the pan between the four toasted tortillas. Top each burrito with cherry tomato quarters and avocado slices. Season to taste with salt and pepper before garnishing with fresh coriander leaves.

4. Serve the burritos hot, with a drizzling of sriracha sauce.

# SPICY BREAKFAST CHILAQUILES

COOK TIME: 30 MINS | MAKES: 4-6 SERVINGS

## INGREDIENTS:

- 12 corn wraps
- 2 tsp. extra-virgin olive oil
- 1 block medium-firm tofu
- 1 tsp. garlic powder
- 2 tsp. tamari sauce
- 1/4 cup nutritional yeast
- 1-2 jalapeños, chopped (extra for garnish)
- 1 bell pepper, any color, chopped
- 1/2 medium shallot, chopped
- 2-3 cups kale, chopped
- 2 tsp. crushed garlic
- 1/4 cup vegetable stock
- 2 1/2 cups store-bought salsa Verde
- Fresh coriander leaves, chopped (for garnish)
- Avocado, sliced (for garnish)
- Salsa Fresca (for garnish)

## DIRECTIONS:

1. Set the oven to preheat to 400°F, with the wire rack in the center of the oven.

2. Cut each wrap into 8 triangles, and arrange the slices on a dry baking sheet. Bake in the oven for 15-20 minutes until the slices are lightly toasted. They may harden slightly during this time.

3. Meanwhile, in a large frying pan over medium heat, heat 1 teaspoon of olive oil. When the oil is nice and hot, break the tofu up into the pan. Don't worry if it seems a bit runny, this will mimic the texture of real scrambled eggs. Add the garlic powder and tamari, stirring for 1-2 minutes, or until about half the water from the tofu has evaporated. Add the nutritional yeast, and stir until properly incorporated. Scrape the cooked tofu into a bowl, and tent to keep warm.

4. Use a paper towel to wipe out the pan, and then heat the final teaspoon of oil over medium heat. When the oil is nice and hot, fry the jalapeños, bell pepper, and shallots for 3-5 minutes, or until the shallots begin to caramelize. Stir in the kale and garlic, allowing the flavors to meld for 30 seconds.

5. Once the wrap triangles are nicely toasted, crumble about half of them into the pan, along with 2 tablespoons of the stock and 1 cup of salsa. Stir until everything is properly combined. Scoop half of the cooked tofu over everything in the pan, before layering the remaining wraps over the top. Add the remaining tofu, salsa, and stock over the wraps in a single layer.

6. Gently tilt the pan from side to side to ensure that all of the stock and juices are evenly distributed. This will soften the bits of wrap that hardened in the oven. Allow to simmer for 5 minutes – the juices should evaporate.

7. Serve hot, garnished with extra jalapeños, coriander leaves, avocado, and salsa Fresca.

# FIERY VEGAN BREAKFAST TACOS

COOK TIME: 15 MINS | MAKES: 8 SERVINGS

## INGREDIENTS:

- 2 tsp. dried oregano
- 1 tbsp. chili powder
- 1 tbsp. ground cumin
- 2 tsp. olive oil
- 1 shallot, finely chopped
- 1 red bell pepper, diced
- 2 cups broccoli florets, chopped into bite-sized pieces
- 4 tsp. crushed garlic
- 2 jalapeños, finely chopped
- 1 block extra-firm tofu
- 2 tbsp. freshly squeezed lime juice
- 2-3 tsp. kikkoman soy sauce
- 1/3 cup nutritional yeast
- 1 carrot, shredded
- 2 tsp. sriracha sauce
- 8 corn wraps, warmed (for serving)

## DIRECTIONS:

1. In a small glass bowl, whisk together the oregano, chili powder, and ground cumin. Set aside.

2. In a large frying pan, heat the olive oil. When the oil is nice and hot, fry the shallots for 3-5 minutes, or until they caramelize around the edges. Stir in the bell pepper and broccoli for 3-4 minutes, or until the broccoli is fork-tender but still crisp. Add the garlic and jalapeños, stirring for 30 seconds and allowing the flavors to meld.

3. Meanwhile, use your hands to press as much water from the tofu as possible. Break the tofu up into medium-sized pieces – you don't want the pieces to be too small, as they will shrink while they cook. Add the crumbled tofu to the pan, and stir for 2-3 minutes until properly incorporated. If the water evaporates too quickly, stir in a few splashes of filtered water.

4. Stir in the lime juice and soy sauce, then add the spice mixture and stir until properly combined. Add the nutritional yeast and shredded carrots. Stir the pan for about 2 minutes, allowing the flavors to meld. Lastly, stir in the sriracha sauce.

5. Divided the filling between the warmed wraps, and serve.

# VERY BERRY VANILLA PANCAKES

COOK TIME: 28 MINS | MAKES: 14 SERVINGS

## INGREDIENTS:

- 1/2 tsp. kosher salt
- 1 cup oat flour, spooned and leveled
- 1 cup all-purpose flour, spooned and leveled
- 2 1/3 cups almond milk
- 2 tsp. pure vanilla essence
- 1/4 cup unsweetened apple sauce
- 3 1/2 tsp. sunflower oil
- 1 1/2 cups strawberry jam
- Vegan icing sugar for dusting
- Sliced strawberries for serving

## DIRECTIONS:

1. Set the oven to preheat to 225°F, with the wire rack in the center of the oven.

2. Whisk the salt, oat flour, and all-purpose flour together in a mixing bowl. Gradually stir in the milk, then whisk in the vanilla essence and apple sauce until you have a lump-free batter.

3. In a large frying pan over medium heat, heat 1/4 teaspoon of sunflower oil.

4. When the oil is nice and hot, scoop 1/4 cup of the batter into the pan, swirling the pan as you pour to evenly distribute the batter. Cook the pancake for 1 minute and 30 seconds, or until the edges begin to brown. Flip the pancake, and cook for an additional 30 seconds. Transfer the cooked pancake to a plate, and store in the preheated oven while you cook the rest of the pancakes.

5. Repeat the process with the remaining batter, adding additional oil between pancakes, as needed.

6. Spoon about 2 tablespoons of jam onto each pancake before rolling it up. Plate the rolled-up pancakes, dust with icing sugar, and garnish with strawberry slices before serving.

# CINNAMON & CHOCOLATE BANANA BREAD

COOK TIME: 60 MINS | MAKES: 8 SERVINGS

## INGREDIENTS:

- Vegan-friendly baking spray
- 1/3 cup raw walnuts
- 1 tsp. pure vanilla essence
- 1/2 cup melted coconut oil, slightly cooled
- 3/4 cup brown sugar
- 1 1/2 cups very ripe bananas, mashed
- 3/4 tsp. ground cinnamon
- 1/4 tsp. ground nutmeg
- 3/4 tsp. kosher salt
- 1/2 tsp. baking soda
- 1 1/2 tsp. baking powder
- 2 cups all-purpose flour, spooned and leveled
- 1/2 cup vegan chocolate chips (extra for garnish)

## DIRECTIONS:

1. Set the oven to preheat to 350°F, with the wire rack in the center of the oven. Coat a large bread pan with baking spray, and line with greaseproof paper, allowing the edges to hang over and act as handles.

2. Fan the walnuts out on a clean baking sheet, and roast in the oven for 10 minutes until the edges have crisped. Allow the nuts to cool on the counter before coarsely chopping.

3. Whisk together the vanilla, coconut oil, sugar, and mashed bananas in a large mixing bowl. Use a wooden spoon to stir in the cinnamon, nutmeg, salt, baking soda, baking powder, and all-purpose flour, until properly combined into a thick batter. Gently fold in the chocolate chips and toasted walnuts.

4. Scrape the batter into the prepared bread pan in an even layer before garnishing with the extra chocolate chips. Place the pan in the oven for 57-60 minutes, or until an inserted skewer comes out clean with only a few moist crumbs.

5. Transfer the bread pan to a cooling rack for 20 minutes before using the paper handles to unmold the loaf. Allow the loaf to cool completely on the counter before slicing.

# BREAKFAST BAGEL SANDWICHES

COOK TIME: 10-15 MINS | MAKES: 2 SERVINGS

## INGREDIENTS:

- 2 vegan sausage patties
- 1 tbsp. extra-virgin olive oil
- 1/4 cup shallots, diced
- 1/4 tsp. Himalayan black salt
- 1/4 tsp. garlic powder
- 1/4 tsp. ground turmeric
- 1/2 cup extra-firm tofu, drained and crumbled
- 1/2 cup baby spinach
- 1/4 cup heirloom tomatoes, chopped
- 2 slices vegan cheese
- 1 tbsp. filtered water
- 2 vegan bagels, toasted and sliced
- Hot sauce for serving

## DIRECTIONS:

1. Cook the patties according to the instructions on the packaging, and set aside.

2. Heat the olive oil in a medium-sized frying pan over medium-low heat. When the oil is nice and hot, fry the shallots for 3 minutes, or until translucent. Stir in the salt, garlic powder, turmeric, and crumbled tofu for about 3 minutes until heated through. The tofu should turn yellow from the turmeric when mixed.

3. Stir in the baby spinach and chopped tomatoes, until all of the ingredients are properly combined and the spinach has reduced in size. Shift the tofu and vegetables to the side, and add the cooked patties to the pan. Heap the tofu and spinach on top of each patty before topping with a slice of vegan cheese.

4. Drizzle the filtered water into the pan around the patties, and immediately cover with a fitted lid. Allow the steam to melt the cheese for 40-60 seconds.

5. When the cheese has melted, place each patty onto a bagel half, and drizzle with hot sauce before covering with the other bagel halves and serving.

# STRAWBERRY CORNMEAL WAFFLES

COOK TIME: 30 MINS | MAKES: 4 SERVINGS

## INGREDIENTS:

- 1/2 tsp. pure vanilla essence
- 1/4 cup freshly squeezed orange juice
- 2-4 tbsp. white sugar
- 1 lb. strawberries, stemmed and chopped
- 1 tsp. freshly squeezed lemon juice
- 2 cups soy milk
- 1/8 tsp. ground nutmeg
- 1/8 tsp. ground cinnamon
- 1/2 tsp. kosher salt
- 1 1/2 tbsp. baking powder
- 2 tbsp. organic dark brown sugar
- 1 cup whole-wheat flour
- 1 1/2 cups cornmeal
- 2 tbsp. sunflower oil
- Vegan-friendly cooking spray

## DIRECTIONS:

1. In a small pot over medium-low heat, stir together the vanilla, orange juice, white sugar, and chopped strawberries. Stir the mixture until you are able to maintain a gentle simmer. Simmer the pot for 15-20 minutes, while stirring at regular intervals to prevent burning. Remove the pot from the heat when the liquid reduces and the syrup thickens. Allow the pot to cool on the counter while you prepare the waffles.

2. In a small glass bowl, whisk together the lemon juice and soy milk. Set aside, and preheat the waffle iron.

3. In a large mixing bowl, whisk together the nutmeg, cinnamon, salt, baking powder, brown sugar, flour, and cornmeal. Create a well in the center of the flour mixture, and add the soy milk and lemon juice, along with the sunflower oil. Use a wooden spoon to mix the batter until it is nearly lump-free, and all of the flour is properly incorporated.

4. Generously coat the waffle iron with cooking spray. Divide the batter into 4 parts, and scoop each portion onto a waffle mold. You will need to do more than 1 batch if you only have a single-mold iron. Cook the waffles until the edges become golden and crispy.

5. Serve the waffles hot with the cooled syrup.

# AUTUMN-SPICED OATMEAL BREAD

COOK TIME: 38-40 MINS | MAKES: 12 SERVINGS

## INGREDIENTS:

- 1/4 cup filtered water
- 2 tbsp. flax meal
- 3/4 tsp. kosher salt
- 1/2 tsp. baking powder
- 1/2 tsp. baking soda
- 1 tsp. pumpkin pie spice
- 1/8 tsp. ground cinnamon
- 1/8 tsp. ground nutmeg
- 1 cup all-purpose flour
- 1 1/4 cups traditional rolled oats
- 3/4 cup dried cranberries, roughly chopped
- 1 tbsp. pure vanilla essence
- 1/2 cup unsweetened apple sauce
- 3/4 cup canned pumpkin purée
- 3/4 cup organic dark brown sugar

## DIRECTIONS:

1. Set the oven to preheat to 350°F, with the wire rack in the center of the oven. Line a bread pan with grease-proof paper, allowing the edges to hang over the pan and act as handles.

2. In a medium-sized glass bowl, whisk together the filtered water and flax meal. Set the bowl aside, and allow the mixture to thicken for 5 minutes on the counter.

3. Whisk together the salt, baking powder, baking soda, pumpkin pie spice, cinnamon, nutmeg, flour, and rolled oats. Use a wooden spoon to stir in the cranberries, vanilla, apple sauce, pumpkin purée, and dark brown sugar, until you have a lump-free batter.

4. Scrape the batter into the prepared bread pan in an even layer. Bake in the oven for 38-40 minutes, or until an inserted skewer comes out clean, and the top is golden brown. Allow the pan to cool completely on the counter, before using the paper handles to lift the loaf out of the pan. Slice the loaf into 12 sections, and serve.

**Quick Tip:**
Replace the dried cranberries with 1/2 cup of fresh cranberries for a prettier loaf with a tart taste.

# SPRING ONION & EDAMAME RICE BOWL

COOK TIME: 0 MINS | MAKES: 4-6 SERVINGS

## INGREDIENTS:

- 1 tsp. kikkoman soy sauce
- 4 tsp. toasted sesame oil
- 2 tbsp. freshly squeezed orange juice
- 1/4 cup rice vinegar
- 1 cup spring onions, sliced
- 4 cups shelled edamame beans
- Cooked basmati rice (enough for 4 bowls)
- 1/3 cup almond slivers, lightly toasted

## DIRECTIONS:

1. In a high-powered food processor, pulse the soy sauce, toasted sesame oil, orange juice, rice vinegar, and spring onions on high until you have a smooth sauce.

2. Divide the cooked rice and edamame beans between 4 serving bowls, and drizzle each bowl with about 1 tablespoon of spring onion sauce. Garnish the bowls with almond slivers for added crunch, and serve.

# VERSATILE OVEN-BAKED PANCAKES

COOK TIME: 12-14 MINS | MAKES: 12 SERVINGS

## INGREDIENTS:

**For the Batter:**
- Vegan-friendly cooking spray
- 1/2 tsp. ground cinnamon
- 1/4 tsp. ground nutmeg
- 1/2 tsp. kosher salt
- 1 tbsp. baking powder
- 1/2 cup organic cane sugar
- 3 cups all-purpose flour
- 2 tsp. pure vanilla essence
- 2 cups unsweetened almond milk

**Chocolate Chip Pancakes:**
- 10 oz. vegan chocolate chips

**Cinnamon Roll Pancakes:**
- 1 tbsp. ground cinnamon
- 1/4 cup organic dark brown sugar
- 3 tbsp. vegan butter, melted

**Berry Pancakes:**
- 2 cups frozen berries of your choice

**Cinnamon Roll Glaze:**
- 1-2 tsp. unsweetened almond milk
- 1 cup vegan icing sugar

**Serving:**
- Pure maple syrup
- Vegan butter

## DIRECTIONS:

1. Set the oven to preheat to 425°F, with the wire rack in the center of the oven. Line a large baking tray with greaseproof paper, allowing the paper to hang over the edges by 1 inch on all sides. Spray the paper with cooking spray, and set aside.

2. In a large mixing bowl, whisk together the cinnamon, nutmeg, salt, baking powder, cane sugar, and flour. Make a well in the center of the flour, and add the vanilla essence and almond milk. Use a wooden spoon to stir the ingredients together until you have an almost lump-free batter. You do not want to overmix the batter. If you are making chocolate chip pancakes, fold in the chocolate chips before spreading the batter onto the baking tray. Simply omit the chocolate chips if using another option.

3. Scrape the batter onto the prepared baking tray in an even layer, and set aside. Choose your favorite topping before baking in the preheated oven.

4. Cinnamon roll pancakes: In a small glass bowl, whisk together cinnamon, brown sugar, and butter. Sprinkle the mixture over the batter on the baking tray, and use a knife to gently draw swirls over the surface.

5. Berry pancakes: Arrange the berries over the batter in an even layer.

6. Once your topping is prepared, bake the pancakes in the oven for 12-14 minutes, or until the edges are golden brown and an inserted toothpick comes out clean.

7. Allow the pancakes to cool slightly before cutting. Serve with pure maple syrup and vegan butter if desired.

8. If making the cinnamon roll pancakes: Place the almond milk and icing sugar in a small glass bowl, and whisk until you have a smooth consistency. Allow the pancakes to cool for 5 minutes before drizzling with the icing mixture. Drizzle with extra glaze before serving if desired.

# COCONUTTY CHIA PUDDING

COOK TIME: 0 MINS | MAKES: 4 SERVINGS

## INGREDIENTS:

- 1/4 tsp. kosher salt
- 1 1/2 tsp. pure vanilla essence
- 2 tbsp. pure maple syrup (extra for serving)
- 1/2 cup chia seeds
- 2 cups unsweetened almond milk (extra if desired)
- 1/4 cup shredded coconut
- 2 cups sliced bananas or strawberries

## DIRECTIONS:

1. In a glass mixing bowl, whisk together the salt, vanilla, maple syrup, chia seeds, and almond milk. Allow the mixture to thicken on the counter for 15 minutes. Whisk again to break up any clumps that may have formed. Seal the bowl with cling wrap, and chill for a minimum of 8 hours, or up to 7 days.

2. When ready to serve, whisk in a bit of extra almond milk, if desired, to make the pudding thinner. Scoop the pudding into 4 serving bowls, and top with shredded coconut and sliced fruit. Serve immediately with an optional drizzling of maple syrup for sweetness, and enjoy.

# SNACKS & LIGHT BITES

# SPICY, OVEN-BAKED BANANA CHIPS

COOK TIME: 20 MINS | MAKES: 4-6 SERVINGS

## INGREDIENTS:

- Vegan-friendly cooking spray
- 1 large green cooking banana
- 2 tbsp. freshly squeezed lemon juice
- 1 tbsp. extra-virgin olive oil
- 1/4 tsp. kosher salt
- 1/4 tsp. cayenne pepper
- 2 tsp. chili powder

## DIRECTIONS:

1. Set the oven to preheat to 400°F, with the wire rack in the center of the oven. Coat a large, rimmed baking sheet with cooking spray.

2. Remove the banana peel, and slice the fruit into thin discs of about 1/8 inch thick.

3. In a medium-sized glass bowl, whisk together the lemon juice and olive oil. Add the banana discs, and use a wooden spoon to gently stir the banana pieces until all of them are evenly coated. Use a slotted spoon to transfer the coated bananas to a clean mixing bowl. Sprinkle the salt, cayenne pepper, and chili powder over the banana discs. Gently stir the bowl until all the pieces are evenly coated in the spices.

4. Fan the coated banana discs out on the prepared baking sheet in a single layer, and bake in the oven for 10 minutes. Turn the banana pieces with a spatula, and bake for an additional 10 minutes, or until the banana discs are a crispy golden brown. Allow the banana chips to cool before serving.

**Quick Tip:**
Banana chips are best consumed on the same day, as they tend to lose their crispness the following day.

# PEANUT-DIPPED SPICY CAULIFLOWER BITES

COOK TIME: 20 MINS | MAKES: 4-6 SERVINGS

## INGREDIENTS:

**Vegan-friendly cooking spray**
- 1/2 cup filtered water
- 1/2 cup all-purpose flour
- 2 lbs. cauliflower florets, chopped into bite-sized pieces
- 1/2 tsp. kikkoman soy sauce
- 1/4 cup rice vinegar
- 1/2-2/3 cup hot sauce
- 2 tsp. extra-virgin olive oil
- 1 English cucumber, sliced into sticks (for serving)

**Peanut Sauce:**
- 1/4 cup plus 2 tbsp. smooth peanut butter
- 1/4 cup warm filtered water
- 1 tsp. agave syrup
- 1 tsp. tamari sauce
- 2 tsp. fresh ginger, grated
- 2 tbsp. freshly squeezed lemon juice
- 2 tbsp. rice vinegar

## DIRECTIONS:

1. Set the oven to preheat to 450°F, with the wire rack in the center of the oven. Generously coat a large, rimmed baking sheet with cooking spray, and set aside.

2. In a medium-sized mixing bowl, whisk together the filtered water and flour until you have a lump-free mixture. Add the florets, and toss until all of the pieces are coated in the flour paste. Fan the coated florets out on the prepared baking sheet, and bake in the oven for 15 minutes, flipping halfway through the cooking time to ensure an even roast.

3. In a small pot over low heat, whisk together the soy sauce, rice vinegar, hot sauce, and olive oil, until the sauce is properly combined and just heated through, but not yet simmering. Turn off the heat, and let the sauce stand while you prepare the rest of the dish.

4. Place the peanut butter and warm filtered water in a glass bowl, and whisk until you have a smooth paste. Whisk in the agave syrup, tamari sauce, fresh ginger, lemon juice, and rice vinegar. Cover the bowl, and chill until the dish is ready to serve.

5. When the cauliflower has been in the oven for 15 minutes, scrape the cooked florets into a large mixing bowl, along with the hot sauce from the pot, and stir to coat. Use tongs to transfer the coated florets back to the oven, and roast for an additional 3 minutes, or until the sauce is heated through and slightly sticky.

6. Plate the roasted cauliflower florets, along with the cucumber sticks, and serve with the peanut sauce on the side for dipping. The extra hot sauce may be used for an additional drizzle over the florets for an added kick.

# VEGAN DIPPING CHEESE

COOK TIME: 10 MINS | MAKES: 2 SERVINGS

## INGREDIENTS:

- 1 cup raw, unsalted cashews
- ½ tsp. kosher salt
- ½ tsp. onion powder
- ¾ tsp. ground turmeric
- 1 tsp. garlic powder
- 1 tsp. sweet smoked paprika
- 2 tbsp. French mustard
- 1 tbsp. white miso seasoning
- ¼ cups tahini sauce
- ¼ cup sauerkraut
- 2 tsp. pure maple syrup
- 1 tbsp. white wine vinegar
- ¼ cup filtered water
- ½ cup vegan lager

## DIRECTIONS:

1. Soak the cashews overnight, or boil them for 10 minutes before you make the recipe. Strain the cashews through a colander set over the sink.

2. Add the softened cashews to a high-powered blender, and add the rest of the ingredients. With the blender on the lowest setting, pulse the ingredients until you have a fine mixture. Scrape down the sides of the blender before pulsing again on high, until you have a cream cheese-like dip.

3. Scrape the mixture into a bowl, and serve alongside your favorite vegetables.

**Quick Tip:**
This cheese dip will thicken when chilled, and can be made 2 days ahead for a lovely spreading cheese.

# EGGLESS FRIED VEGETABLE ROLLS

COOK TIME: 30 MINS | MAKES: 12 SERVINGS

## INGREDIENTS:

- 12 square flour spring roll wrappers
- 2 tbsp. extra-virgin olive oil
- 2 tsp. crushed garlic
- 2 large spring onions, thinly sliced
- 1/2 large shallot, diced
- 1 medium bell pepper, seeded and thinly sliced
- 1 cup carrots, grated
- 5 cups grated cabbage, packed full

- 1 tsp. kosher salt
- 1/4 tsp. freshly ground black pepper
- 1 tbsp. tamari
- 2 tbsp. filtered water
- 1 1/2 tsp. sesame seeds
- Sunflower oil
- Sweet chili sauce for dipping

## DIRECTIONS:

1. The frozen spring roll wrappers should be allowed to defrost at room temperature until fully thawed. Cover the wrappers with a clean kitchen towel that has been slightly dampened, to prevent them from losing too much moisture.

2. Heat the olive oil in a large frying pan over medium-high heat. When the oil is nice and hot, fry the garlic, spring onions, and shallots for 1 minute. Toss in the bell pepper, carrots, and cabbage. Add the salt, pepper, tamari, and filtered water, and stir until all of the ingredients are properly combined. Reduce the heat to medium, and simmer the vegetables for 3-4 minutes, or until the carrots are fork-tender, and the water has evaporated. Add sesame seeds. Remove the pan from the heat, and allow to cool for 5 minutes.

3. Set a bowl of warm filtered water next to a clean work surface. Place a thawed wrapper on the clean surface with one of the corners facing you to make a diamond. Spoon about 2 tablespoons of the filling into the center of the corner nearest you at the bottom of the diamond. You may increase or decrease the amount of filling according to the size of your wrapper.

4. Ensure that you have clean hands, then dip your finger in the warm water and lightly dab each corner of the diamond. This will help seal the roll. Starting at the point with the filling, roll the wrapper up as tight as you can until you reach the center of the diamond. Carefully fold the right and left corners over the filling, gently pressing the moistened corners into the roll. Continue to fold the roll until you reach the end, pressing the moistened tip against the roll to seal it. Repeat the process until you have 12 rolls.

5. Fill a large frying pan to half way with sunflower oil, and heat on high. The oil is ready when the tip of a toothpick immediately begins to sizzle when inserted into the oil. Add half of the spring rolls to the pan, and fry for 2 minutes before flipping, and frying for an additional 2 minutes. Both sides should be golden brown. Transfer the fried spring rolls to a paper towel-lined plate, and repeat with the remaining rolls.

6. Allow the rolls to cool for a few minutes before transferring them to a platter, and serving alongside the dipping sauce.

# CRISPY BAKED SWEET WONTON CUPS

COOK TIME: 25 MINS | MAKES: 12 SERVINGS

## INGREDIENTS:

- 12 square flour spring roll wrappers
- 2 tbsp. extra-virgin olive oil
- 2 tsp. crushed garlic
- 2 large spring onions, thinly sliced
- 1/2 large shallot, diced
- 1 medium bell pepper, seeded and thinly sliced
- 1 cup carrots, grated
- 5 cups grated cabbage, packed full

- 1 tsp. kosher salt
- 1/4 tsp. freshly ground black pepper
- 1 tbsp. tamari
- 2 tbsp. filtered water
- 1 1/2 tsp. sesame seeds
- Sunflower oil
- Sweet chili sauce for dipping

## DIRECTIONS:

1. Allow the wrappers to thaw at room temperature until softened before use. Cover the wrappers with a damp tea towel to prevent them from drying out.

2. Set the oven to preheat to 350°F, with the wire rack in the center of the oven. Lightly coat the inside of each cup of a 12-cup muffin tin with olive oil. Gently press a thawed wrapper into each cup, and bake in the oven for 12 minutes until the wrappers are golden and crispy. Allow the tin to cool on the counter for 5 minutes before unmolding the cups.

3. Press the tofu between two clean kitchen towels for 10 minutes, placing a heavy pot on top to expel any excess water. Slice the drained tofu into 1/2-inch thick cubes before adding them to a mixing bowl, and gently tossing with the salt.

4. In a large frying pan over medium-high heat, heat just enough sunflower oil to cover the bottom of the pan. When the oil is sizzling, add the tofu, and fry for 6 minutes until golden brown, flipping every 2 minutes. Scrape the cooked tofu into a strainer set over the sink to drain any excess water and oil.

5. Discard any excess oil from the pan before adding the shallots and frying for 1 minute, until the shallots just begin to lose their color. Stir in the bell peppers, and fry for 3-4 minutes until they soften. Stir in the tamari and sweet chili sauce for 2 minutes, until the sauce just begins to simmer. Scrape the tofu into the pan, and stir for 2-3 minutes until the sauce thickens. Taste, and adjust the seasoning if desired. Transfer the pan to a wooden chopping board, and allow to cool for 5 minutes.

6. Place the wonton cups on a serving platter, and fill each with 1-1 1/2 tablespoons of the tofu filling. Decorate each cup with toasted sesame seeds and spring onions. Enjoy!

**Quick Tip:**
The wonton cups and filling can be prepared in advance and stored, but should be kept in separate airtight containers until ready to serve. Reheat the filling before building the cups.

# MIDDLE EASTERN OLIVE SALAD

COOK TIME: 0 MINS | MAKES: 2 SERVINGS

## INGREDIENTS:

- 8 fresh mint leaves, torn
- 1/4 cup black olives, pitted
- 1/2 English cucumber, sliced into 1\2-inch rounds
- 1/2 cup baby tomatoes, quartered
- 1/4 tsp. Himalayan salt
- 1/8 tsp. freshly ground black pepper
- 1 tbsp. freshly squeezed lemon juice
- 5 tbsp. extra-virgin olive oil (more if needed)
- 1/4 cup za'atar spice blend
- 1 pita bread, warmed

## DIRECTIONS:

1. Place the mint, olives, cucumber, tomatoes, salt, pepper, lemon juice, and 1 tablespoon of oil in a large mixing bowl, and gently toss to combine.

2. In a small glass bowl, whisk the 4 tablespoons of olive oil with the za'atar. You want a spreadable paste, so if the paste is too thick, whisk in additional oil as needed.

3. Use a serrated knife to slice the warmed pita bread in half.

4. Spread the za'atar paste on the cut side of each pita half, and top with the olive salad. Serve and enjoy.

# SPICY WALNUT & CAULIFLOWER CUPS

COOK TIME: 30 MINS | MAKES: 8-10 SERVINGS

## INGREDIENTS:

- 2 heads cauliflower, cored and chopped into florets
- 1 1\2 tsp. kosher salt
- 1 tsp. ground white pepper
- 2 tbsp. extra-virgin olive oil
- 1 cup walnut halves, coarsely chopped
- 2 tsp. crushed garlic
- 3 spring onions, thinly sliced
- 2 tsp. pure maple syrup
- 2 tsp. white miso paste
- 2 tbsp. hot sauce
- 1 1\2 cups vegan mayonnaise
- 1 tbsp. sesame seeds
- 2 heads iceberg lettuce, leaves separated
- 1 large cucumber, sliced
- 3 large carrots, julienned
- 1/2 cup fresh coriander leaves, chopped

## DIRECTIONS:

1. Set the oven to preheat to 400°F, with the wire rack in the center of the oven. Line a large baking sheet with greaseproof paper.

2. In a large mixing bowl, toss the cauliflower florets with the olive oil, 1 teaspoon of salt, and 1\2 teaspoon pepper. Fan the coated florets out in a single layer on the prepared baking sheet, and bake in the oven for 25-30 minutes, or until the cauliflower is fork-tender and the edges are a crispy golden brown. Allow the cauliflower to cool slightly on the counter.

3. In a large frying pan over medium heat, dry roast the chopped walnuts for 2 minutes, while tossing at regular intervals to prevent burning – about every 30 seconds should do it. Transfer the pan to a wooden chopping board, and allow to stand for 5 minutes.

4. In a medium-sized mixing bowl, whisk together the garlic, two-thirds of the spring onions, the remaining salt and pepper, and the maple syrup, miso paste, hot sauce, and mayonnaise. Gently scrape the cauliflower and walnuts into the bowl of sauce, and stir to combine. Add the remaining spring onions and the sesame seeds, gently stirring to combine.

5. Place about 8 or 10 lettuce leaves in individual serving bowls, and divide the mixture between the leaves. Top with cucumber, carrots, and coriander before serving.

# AVOCADO & KALE EGGLESS ROLLS

COOK TIME: 30 MINS | MAKES: 24 SERVINGS

## INGREDIENTS:

- 6 ripe avocados, halved and pitted
- 1/2 tsp. cayenne pepper
- 2 tsp. toasted sesame oil
- 2 tsp. kosher salt
- 1 lime, juiced
- 1/3 cup fresh coriander leaves, chopped
- 5 tsp. crushed garlic

- 2 tsp. fresh ginger, grated
- 1 bunch kale, stems removed, chopped
- 24 eggless spring roll wrappers
- Sunflower oil
- Vegan-friendly cooking spray
- Sweet chili sauce

## DIRECTIONS:

1. In a large mixing bowl, mash the avocados, along with the cayenne pepper, sesame oil, salt, lime juice, coriander leaves, garlic, and ginger, leaving a few chunks of avocado for texture.

2. Add half of the kale to the bowl and stir to combine, then add the other half and mix. If the wrappers are frozen, allow them to thaw at room temperature until pliable. Cover the wrappers with a damp kitchen towel to prevent them from drying out while they defrost. You may also cover the wrappers with a damp kitchen towel while you work with them. Place a small bowl of warm filtered water beside a clean work surface.

3. Place a thawed wrapper on the clean surface with one of the corners facing you to make a diamond. Spoon about 2 tablespoons of the filling into the center of the corner nearest you at the bottom of the diamond. You may increase or decrease the amount of filling according to the size of your wrapper.

4. Ensuring that you have clean hands, dip your finger in the warm water, and lightly dab each corner of the diamond. This will help seal the roll. Starting at the point with the filling, roll the wrapper up as tight as you can until you reach the center of the diamond. Carefully fold the right and left corners over the filling, gently pressing the moistened corners into the roll. Continue to fold the roll until you reach the end, pressing the moistened tip against the roll to seal. Repeat the process until you have 24 rolls.

5. To fry the rolls: Fill a large frying pan to half way with oil, and heat over high heat. The oil is ready when the tip of a toothpick immediately begins to sizzle when inserted into the oil. Working in batches, fry the rolls for 1-2 minutes per side, before flipping and frying for an additional 1-2 minutes. The rolls should be an even golden brown. Transfer the cooked rolls to a paper towel-lined plate, and repeat the process with the remaining rolls.

6. If baking: Set the oven to preheat to 400°F, with the wire rack in the center of the oven, and line a large, rimmed baking sheet with greaseproof paper. You may need to use more than 1 baking sheet if the rolls do not comfortably fit on a single one. Arrange the rolls on the prepared sheet or sheets, and evenly coat them with cooking spray – this step will allow the rolls to crisp in the oven.

7. Bake the rolls in the oven for 15-20 minutes, or until the rolls are a crispy golden brown. Allow them to cool slightly on the counter.

8. Serve the cooked rolls with sweet chili sauce on the side for dipping.

# OVEN-BAKED VEGAN NACHOS

COOK TIME: 10-12 MINS | MAKES: 6-8 SERVINGS

## INGREDIENTS:

- 12 oz. tortilla chips
- 2.25 0z. Kalamata olives, pitted and sliced
- 1/2 red bell pepper, roughly chopped
- 1/2 cup frozen corn
- 15 oz. black turtle beans, drained and rinsed
- 1 cup red cabbage, shredded
- 1 cup vegan cheese, shredded
- Sliced jalapeños
- Vegan-friendly sour cream
- 1 Hass avocado, peeled and chopped
- 1 cup store-bought salsa
- 3 spring onions, roughly chopped

## DIRECTIONS:

1. Set the oven to preheat to 400°F, with the wire rack in the center of the oven. Line a large, rimmed baking tray with greaseproof paper.

2. Arrange a layer of tortilla chips on the prepared baking tray. Add the olives, bell pepper, corn, beans, and cabbage in a single layer, until the chips are no longer visible. Sprinkle the cheese over everything on the tray.

3. Place the tray in the oven for 10-12 minutes, or until the cheese has melted and the edges of the nachos are a crispy golden brown. If the cheese is not melting to your satisfaction, place the tray beneath the broiler for 1-2 minutes.

4. When the cheese has melted, top the nachos with jalapeños, sour cream, avocado, salsa, and spring onions. Serve hot and enjoy.

# QUICK & EASY PIZZA BITES

COOK TIME: 10-12 MINS | MAKES: 12 SERVINGS

## INGREDIENTS:

- Vegan-friendly cooking spray
- 2 large flour wraps
- 3/4 cup store-bought pizza sauce
- 3/4 cup vegan mozzarella
- 1/3 cup Kalamata olives, pitted and halved
- Italian seasoning
- Pizza toppings of your choice

## DIRECTIONS:

1. Set the oven to preheat to 425°F, with the wire rack in the center of the oven. Coat a 12-cup muffin tin with cooking spray.

2. Place the wraps on a clean surface, and use a cookie cutter or the rim of a can to cut 12 circles. Always ensure that anything you are using to cook with has been sanitized beforehand. Keep the scraps for another use.

3. Carefully press a circle into each muffin cup, taking care not to tear the wrap circles. Lightly spray each circle with cooking spray. Spoon 1 tablespoon of the pizza sauce into each cup, followed by 1 tablespoon of cheese per cup. Garnish with olives and Italian seasoning. Top the pizza bites with any other vegan toppings of your choice, if desired.

4. Place the pizza bites in the oven for 10-12 minutes, or until the cheese is bubbly and the edges of the cups are lightly toasted. Unmold the bites, and serve warm.

**Quick Tip:**
The cuttings from the wraps can be used to make chips or crispy salad toppings. Simply fry the cuttings in hot oil, and season to taste with salt and pepper.

# CRUNCHY FRIED CHICKPEAS

COOK TIME: 12-15 MINS | MAKES: 6 SERVINGS

## INGREDIENTS:

- 30 oz. canned chickpeas, rinsed and drained
- 1/2 tsp. kosher salt
- 1/4 tsp. white pepper
- 1 tsp. refined sugar
- 1 tsp. sweet smoked paprika
- 1 cup extra-virgin olive oil

## DIRECTIONS:

1. Place the drained chickpeas between two clean kitchen towels, and gently rub to ensure they are properly dried – this will help make the chickpeas extra crunchy.

2. In a small glass bowl, whisk together the salt, pepper, sugar, and paprika, and set aside.

3. Heat the oil in a large pot over high heat. The oil is ready when it just begins to smoke. Watch the temperature – you want the oil to remain hot throughout the frying process. Place the chickpeas in the oil, and fry for 12-15 minutes or until the peas are crispy. Use a slotted spoon to transfer the chickpeas to a paper towel-lined plate. To check the crispness, place 2 or 3 peas on a plate, and allow them to cool slightly before tasting. If the peas are not crunchy enough for you, fry them for another 2-3 minutes.

4. Fan the fried chickpeas out on a baking tray, and allow them to cool completely before tossing them in a bowl with the spice mixture, and serving.

**Quick Tip:**
Crunchy chickpeas are best consumed quickly, as they tend to lose their crispness after about 2 hours at room temperature.

# ZESTY POPPING PEPPER CAULIFLOWER WINGS!

COOK TIME: 30 MINS | MAKES: 4 SERVINGS

## INGREDIENTS:

**Cauliflower:**
- 1/2 tsp. kosher salt
- 2 tsp. onion powder
- 2 tsp. garlic powder
- 1 tbsp. lemon-pepper seasoning
- 1 tbsp. nutritional dry yeast
- 1 tbsp. corn flour
- 1 cup all-purpose flour
- 1 1/2 cups unsweetened almond milk
- 4 cups cauliflower florets, patted dry

- Vegan-friendly cooking spray (if baking)
- Sunflower oil (if frying)

**Sauce:**
- 1/2 cup almond butter
- 2 lemons, zested and juiced
- 4 tsp. crushed garlic
- 1/4 cup nutritional yeast
- 1/2 tsp. flaky sea salt
- 1 tsp. freshly ground black pepper

## DIRECTIONS:

1. Place the salt, onion powder, garlic powder, lemon-pepper seasoning, yeast, corn flour, and all-purpose flour in a large bowl, and mix until all of the ingredients are properly combined. Whisk in the milk until you have a lump-free batter. Make sure that the cauliflower is completely dry before adding the florets to the batter, as it will not stick if they are wet. Toss until all the florets are evenly coated in the batter.

2. Set the oven to preheat to 425°F, with the wire rack in the center of the oven, and line a large, rimmed baking sheet with greaseproof paper. Coat the paper with a generous amount of cooking spray.

3. Use tongs to arrange the coated florets on the prepared baking sheet, making sure that they do not touch. This will ensure that the florets crisp evenly. Bake the cauliflower in the oven for 20-25 minutes, or until it is a crispy golden brown.

4. If you wish to fry the florets, heat the sunflower oil in a large frying pan over high heat. The oil should come to about halfway up the side of the pan. It is ready to be used when the tip of an inserted toothpick immediately begins to sizzle. Fry the coated florets in batches for 2-3 minutes per side, then transfer the fried cauliflower to a paper towel-lined baking sheet and keep warm in the oven.

5. In a small pot over low heat, heat the almond butter until just beginning to soften, but not melted. Remove the pot from the heat, and whisk in the lemon zest and juice. Add the garlic, yeast, salt, and pepper, whisking until you have a creamy sauce.

6. Add the crispy cauliflower wings to a large mixing bowl, and gently toss them with the lemon and pepper sauce. Plate the coated wings, and serve hot with any extra sauce drizzled over the top.

**Quick Tip:**
If using gluten-free flour, allow the batter to sit for 5 minutes before adding the florets to the bowl. If using a flour blend, one with rice flour will work best to give the wings a crispier coating.

# CRUNCHY OVEN-BAKED ZUCCHINI CHIPS

COOK TIME: 30-40 MINS | MAKES: 4-6 SERVINGS

## INGREDIENTS:

- Vegan-friendly cooking spray
- Kosher salt
- 1/4 tsp. garlic powder
- 1/4 tsp. sweet smoked paprika
- 1 tbsp. all-purpose flour
- 1 medium zucchini, about 4 inches long and 1 1/2 inches wide

## DIRECTIONS:

1. Set the oven to preheat to 350°F, with the wire rack in the center of the oven. Coat a large, rimmed baking tray with greaseproof paper.

2. In a large mixing bowl, whisk together the salt, garlic powder, paprika, and flour. Set the bowl aside while you chop the zucchini.

3. Use a sharp knife to slice the zucchini into discs only slightly bigger than a quarter. The chips may burn quickly if sliced too thin. Use paper towels to dab any excess liquid from the zucchini discs before adding them to the bowl of spices. Toss the bowl until all of the discs are evenly coated in spices.

4. Arrange the zucchini on the prepared baking tray in a single layer before giving everything a coat of cooking spray. Bake in the oven for 30-40 minutes, flipping the discs at 10-minute intervals until the chips are a crunchy golden brown. Check back regularly, as these chips tend to burn very quickly if not monitored properly.

5. Allow the chips to cool slightly before serving. Enjoy the crunchiness!

**Quick Tip:**
These chips are best eaten on the same day, as they tend to lose their crispness if left overnight.

# FIERY GARLIC-PICKLED CARROTS

COOK TIME: 5-10 MINS | MAKES: 4-6 SERVINGS

## INGREDIENTS:

- 1/4 tsp. kosher salt
- 2 tsp. crushed garlic
- 1/4 cup shallots, thinly sliced
- 1/4 tsp. freshly ground black pepper
- 1/2 tsp. ground cumin seeds
- 1 whole bay leaf
- 1 tsp. dried oregano
- 1/2 cup apple cider vinegar
- 3/4 cup distilled white vinegar
- 2 jalapeños, sliced into 1/4-inch rounds
- 1/2 lb. carrots, sliced into 1/4-inch rounds

## DIRECTIONS:

1. In a medium pot over medium heat, whisk together the salt, garlic, shallots, pepper, cumin, bay leaf, oregano, apple cider vinegar, and white vinegar, then bring the mixture to a boil. Once the sauce begins to boil, lower the heat to maintain a gentle simmer.

2. Add the jalapeños and carrots, simmering for 3-5 minutes until the carrots have softened slightly, but still have a bit of crunch.

3. Immediately pour the mixture into a large glass jar, and seal with a tight-fitting lid. Let the jar stand for a minimum of 8 hours or overnight. Unseal the jar and serve.

**Quick Tip:**
An opened jar can be kept in the refrigerator for no more than 3 weeks.

# CRISPY CAULIFLOWER BUFFALO BITES

COOK TIME: 15-20 MINS | MAKES: 4-6 SERVINGS

## INGREDIENTS:

**Buffalo sauce:**
- 1/4 cup coconut oil
- 2 tsp. apple cider vinegar
- 1 tbsp. packed organic dark brown sugar
- 1/2 cup sriracha sauce

**Cauliflower:**
- Sunflower oil for frying
- Kosher salt
- Freshly ground black pepper
- 1/4 cup cornmeal
- 3/4 cup corn starch
- 1 tbsp. sriracha sauce
- 2/3 cup coconut milk

- 1 lb. cauliflower florets, chopped into 1 1/2-inch pieces

**Ranch Dressing:**
- 1/8 tsp. kosher salt
- 1/8 tsp. freshly ground black pepper
- 1/4 tsp. garlic powder
- 1 1/2 tsp. fresh dill, minced
- 1 1/2 tsp. fresh chives, minced
- 1 tsp. white wine vinegar
- 2 tablespoons unsweetened plain coconut milk yogurt
- 1/2 cup vegan mayonnaise

## DIRECTIONS:

1. In a small pot over low heat, melt the coconut oil. Add the apple cider vinegar, brown sugar, and sriracha sauce, whisking to combine. Remove the pot from the stove when all of the ingredients are properly incorporated into the sauce, and set aside.

2. Prepare a serving platter by placing three layers of paper towels on it to absorb the oil. Fill a large pot to about 1 1/2 inches deep with sunflower oil, and heat over medium-high heat.

3. Meanwhile, in a small glass bowl, whisk together 1/2 teaspoon salt, 1/4 teaspoon pepper, the cornmeal, and the corn starch. In a separate large mixing bowl, whisk together the sriracha sauce and coconut milk. Add the cauliflower florets to the sauce mixture, and stir to combine. Scrape the corn starch mixture over the cauliflower, and use a rubber spatula to gently stir the ingredients until the florets are evenly coated in the sauce and corn starch mixture.

4. When the oil is piping hot, divide the cauliflower into 2 batches. Fry each batch for about 3 minutes, or until the florets are a crispy golden brown. Gently stir the oil as the florets fry, to prevent them from sticking together. Transfer the cooked florets to the paper towel-lined platter, and repeat the process until all of the florets have been fried.

5. Add the fried florets to a large mixing bowl, and toss with 1/2 cup of the buffalo sauce. Transfer the coated florets to a clean serving platter, and tent to keep warm.

6. To make the ranch dressing, place all of the ingredients in a medium-sized mixing bowl, and whisk until you have a lump-free sauce.

7. Serve the platter of crispy cauliflower florets with the homemade ranch dressing and extra buffalo sauce on the side.

# SALADS & BOWLS

# TOSSED CHICKPEA GARDEN SALAD

COOK TIME: 2 MINS | MAKES: 4-6 SERVINGS

## INGREDIENTS:

- 30 oz. canned chickpeas, drained and rinsed
- 2 tbsp. freshly squeezed lemon juice
- 1/4 cup extra-virgin olive oil
- Pinch cayenne pepper
- 3/4 tsp. kosher salt
- 1/2 tsp. freshly ground black pepper
- 1/2 cup black olives, pitted and roughly chopped
- 1 cup baby arugula, roughly chopped
- 3 cups carrots, peeled and shredded

## DIRECTIONS:

1. Place the drained chickpeas in a large, microwave-safe mixing bowl, and microwave on high for about 2 minutes until the chickpeas are heated through. Add the lemon juice, olive oil, cayenne pepper, salt, and pepper to the hot chickpeas, and stir to combine. Cover the bowl, and allow the chickpeas to stand at room temperature for half an hour.

2. After 30 minutes, add the olives, baby arugula, and carrots to the bowl, tossing to combine. Season to taste with additional salt and pepper if desired, and serve.

# FRESH HERB & SPUD SALAD

COOK TIME: 25 MINS | MAKES: 4 SERVINGS

## INGREDIENTS:

- 1 lb. baby potatoes, skin on
- 1/4 tsp. Himalayan salt
- 1/2 tsp. sweet smoked paprika
- 3 tbsp. extra-virgin olive oil (divided)
- 1 tsp. freshly squeezed lemon juice
- 1 tbsp. filtered water
- 2 tbsp. apple cider vinegar
- 2 tsp. crushed garlic
- 1/2 cup spring onions, sliced
- 1/2 cup fresh parsley, diced
- Kosher salt (optional)
- Freshly ground black pepper (optional)

## DIRECTIONS:

1. Set the oven to preheat to 400°F, with the wire rack in the center of the oven.

2. If the potatoes are not already bite-sized, chop them in half lengthwise or slice them into quarters. Add the potatoes to a large mixing bowl, and toss them with the salt, paprika, and 1 tablespoon of olive oil until evenly coated. Fan the coated potatoes out on a large baking tray, and bake in the oven for 12 minutes before flipping, and baking for an additional 13 minutes.

3. In a high-powered food processor, pulse the remaining olive oil, lemon juice, filtered water, vinegar, garlic, spring onions, and parsley on high, until you have a smooth paste.

4. When the potatoes are fork-tender, allow them to cool on the counter for 10 minutes before placing them in a large mixing bowl. Scrape the sauce from the blender into the bowl, and toss until all of the potatoes are evenly coated in the sauce. Season the salad with extra salt and pepper if desired. Cover the bowl, and chill for a minimum of 1 hour before serving.

5. The salad can be served hot, cold, or at room temperature.

# ROASTED BEET & QUINOA SALAD

COOK TIME: 35 MINS | MAKES: 4 SERVINGS

## INGREDIENTS:

**Dressing:**
- 1/4 cup extra-virgin olive oil
- 3 tbsp. balsamic vinegar
- 1 tsp. French mustard
- 2 tbsp. diced shallots

**Salad:**
- 1 1/2 cups beets, peeled and chopped
- 2 tsp. extra-virgin olive oil
- 1 tsp. balsamic vinegar
- Himalayan salt
- 2 cups filtered water
- 1 cup quinoa, rinsed
- 1 cup baby spinach, stems removed, chopped
- 1/4 cup fresh basil leaves, diced
- Freshly ground black pepper

## DIRECTIONS:

1. Set the oven to preheat to 400°F, with the wire rack in the center of the oven, and set a large, rimmed baking tray on the counter.

2. In a small glass bowl, whisk together the olive oil, balsamic vinegar, mustard, and shallots. Set aside.

3. In a large mixing bowl, use a wooden spoon to coat the chopped beets with the olive oil, vinegar, and a pinch of salt. Scrape the mixture onto the baking tray, and bake in the oven for 10 minutes before flipping, and baking for an additional 10 minutes.

4. Meanwhile, bring the water to a rolling boil over medium heat. When the water is boiling, add the quinoa, and lower the heat to maintain a gentle simmer for 15 minutes. Stir the quinoa at regular intervals to prevent burning, until it is done to your liking. Drain any excess water, and scrape the cooked quinoa into a large mixing bowl. Add the baby spinach and stir – the hot quinoa will wilt the spinach as you mix it through. Add the basil leaves, and stir to combine.

5. Taste the quinoa, and season with additional salt and pepper. Add the roasted beets, and use a rubber spatula to stir the ingredients together. Serve the quinoa and beets warm or chilled.

# DECADENT & CRUNCHY CHOPPED SALAD

COOK TIME: 0 MINS | MAKES: 2 SERVINGS

## INGREDIENTS:

- 1/2 tsp. onion powder
- 1 tsp. garlic powder
- 1 lemon, juiced
- 2 tbsp. kikkoman soy sauce
- 2 tbsp. balsamic vinegar
- 1/4 cup filtered water (more if needed)
- 1/4 cup extra-virgin olive oil
- 1/2 cup tahini sauce
- 1/2 tsp. dried parsley
- 2 cups baby spinach, roughly chopped
- 2 cups iceberg lettuce, roughly chopped
- 1/4 cup green olives, pitted and chopped
- 1 Granny Smith apple, cored and chopped
- 1/4 cup walnuts, roughly chopped
- 1/2 cup carrots, shredded
- 1/2 cup cucumber, roughly chopped
- 1/2 cup cherry tomatoes, halved
- 1 cup extra-firm tofu, chopped into 1/2-inch cubes
- 1 tsp. hemp seeds
- 2 tbsp. dried cranberries

## DIRECTIONS:

1. In a high-powered food processor, pulse the onion powder, garlic powder, lemon juice, soy sauce, balsamic vinegar, water, olive oil, and tahini for 1-2 minutes, until you have a completely lump-free dressing. You may add a tablespoon of extra water at a time to reach the desired consistency. Add the dried parsley, and pulse for about 10-15 seconds until the parsley is incorporated, but not entirely blended in.

2. Divide the spinach, lettuce, olives, apple, walnuts, carrots, cucumber, cherry tomatoes, and tofu between two serving bowls, and toss each bowl until all of the ingredients are properly combined.

3. Top each bowl with 1/2 teaspoon of hemp seeds and 1 tablespoon of dried cranberries. Drizzle a generous amount of dressing over each bowl, and serve.

**Quick Tip:**
Any leftover dressing can be refrigerated in an airtight container for no more than 3 weeks.

# PEPPERY LEMON CHICKPEA SALAD

COOK TIME: 0 MINS | MAKES: 8 SERVINGS

## INGREDIENTS:

**Dressing:**
- 1/2 tsp. freshly ground black pepper
- 1/2 tsp. French mustard
- 1/2 tsp. dried tarragon
- 2 tbsp. freshly squeezed lemon juice
- 2 cups vegan classic herb ranch dressing

**Salad:**
- 1 cup fresh basil leaves, chopped
- 1 Granny Smith apple, peeled, cored, and diced
- 1 cup baby tomatoes, halved
- 1 cup crumbled tofu, raw or toasted
- 1 cup plant-based vegan bacon
- 1 small uncooked beet, peeled and shredded
- 1/2 cup pepperoncini peppers, diced
- 2 carrots, shredded
- 14 oz. artichoke hearts, drained and diced
- 1 1/2 cups cooked chickpeas, rinsed, and drained
- 1 English cucumber, thinly sliced
- 1 cup toasted walnuts
- 1/2 cup fried shallots
- 2 cups baby arugula, roughly chopped
- 2 heads iceberg lettuce, thinly sliced

## DIRECTIONS:

1. In a medium-sized mixing bowl, whisk together the pepper, mustard, tarragon, lemon juice, and ranch dressing, until all of the ingredients are properly combined. Seal the bowl, and chill immediately.

2. In a large salad bowl, toss the salad ingredients together until properly combined.

3. Scrape half of the chilled dressing onto the salad, and toss to evenly coat all of the salad ingredients. Add a little more, as desired, and toss. Stack the dressed salad in bowls and serve immediately.

**Quick Tip:**
Any leftover dressing can be refrigerated in an airtight container for no more than 7 days.

# CRUNCHY VEG & VERMICELLI SALAD

COOK TIME: 0 MINS | MAKES: 3 SERVINGS

## INGREDIENTS:

- 1.8 oz. dried rice vermicelli noodles
- 1 bird's eye chili, thinly sliced
- 1 tsp. crushed garlic
- 1 tbsp. extra-virgin olive oil
- 2 tsp. organic dark brown sugar
- 2 tbsp. rice vinegar
- 2 tbsp. tamari
- 2 tbsp. roasted peanuts, chopped (more for garnish)
- 1 packed tbsp. fresh mint leaves, chopped
- 1 tbsp. fresh coriander leaves, chopped (more for garnish)
- 1 spring onion, thinly sliced
- 1 small carrot, peeled and thinly sliced
- 1/2 small red bell pepper, thinly sliced
- 1 cup cabbage, shredded

## DIRECTIONS:

1. Place the dried noodles in a large glass bowl, and cover with boiling water. Place a lid or plate over the bowl, and allow the noodles to soak in the boiling water for 6-7 minutes, or until they are cooked through but slightly chewy. Pour the noodles into a strainer set over the sink to drain. Transfer them to a large bowl, and use kitchen scissors to cut them into small bites about 2-inches long.

2. In a small glass bowl, whisk together the bird's eye chili, garlic, olive oil, brown sugar, rice vinegar, and tamari. Taste the sauce, and adjust the seasoning as desired.

3. Place the roasted peanuts, mint leaves, coriander leaves, spring onion, carrots, bell pepper, and cabbage in a large mixing bowl, and toss to combine. Add the noodle pieces and toss again, then add the dressing, and toss until everything is evenly coated. Cover the bowl with cling wrap, and chill for 30 minutes.

4. Once the salad is nicely chilled, garnish with extra peanuts and coriander leaves if desired, and serve.

**Quick Tip:**
Any leftover salad can be refrigerated in an airtight container for no more than 3 days.

# FULLY LOADED AVO BOWLS

COOK TIME: 0 MINS | MAKES: 2 SERVINGS

## INGREDIENTS:

- 3 cups baby spinach, stems removed
- 1 tsp. balsamic vinegar
- 2 tsp. extra -virgin olive oil
- 1 large Hass avocado, peeled, pitted, and halved
- 1 tbsp. shallots, minced
- 1/4 cup heirloom tomatoes, diced
- 1/4 cup English cucumber, diced
- 1/4 cup yellow bell pepper, diced
- 1/4 cup hummus
- 1/4 cup cooked quinoa
- 1/2 lemon, juiced
- 1/4 tsp. Himalayan salt
- 1/4 tsp. freshly ground black pepper
- Pepitas (for garnish)
- Sweet smoked paprika (for garnish)

## DIRECTIONS:

1. Tear the baby spinach into bite-sized pieces, and place in a large bowl. Drizzle the balsamic vinegar and olive oil over the torn baby spinach, and use clean hands to massage the mixture into the leaves for about 1 minute. The leaves should soften slightly during this time.

2. Spoon the spinach into 2 serving bowls, and place 1 avocado half on each bed of leaves.

3. In the same bowl you used to massage the baby spinach, use a wooden spoon to combine the shallots, tomatoes, cucumber, bell pepper, hummus, quinoa, lemon juice, salt, and pepper.

4. When the ingredients are properly combined, divide the mixture, and spoon it onto the avocados, allowing it to spill over the sides. Garnish the bowls with pepitas and a sprinkling of sweet smoked paprika before serving.

# SPICY, THAI-INSPIRED PUMPKIN STEW

COOK TIME: 40-50 MINS | MAKES: 4-6 SERVINGS

## INGREDIENTS:

- 2 tbsp. extra-virgin olive oil
- 4 cups pumpkin, peeled, seeded, and cubed (bite-sized pieces)
- 1/2 shallot, thinly sliced
- 2 red bell peppers, stemmed, seeded, and julienned
- 3 tbsp. vegan red curry paste
- 3 Thai lime leaves
- 2 dried Thai red chilis
- 1 cup green beans, trimmed and chopped (2-inch pieces)
- 14 oz. canned full-fat coconut milk
- 1 cup frozen green peas
- 1 tsp. kosher salt
- 1 lime, juiced
- 1-2 tbsp. coconut sugar
- 1 tbsp. tamari
- 1/2 cup fresh basil leaves
- Cooked basmati rice (for serving)
- Fresh coriander leaves (for garnish)

## DIRECTIONS:

1. In a large pot over medium-high heat, heat the olive oil. When the oil is nice and hot, fry the pumpkin cubes for 5-6 minutes, or until they are fork-tender and slightly toasted. Add the shallots and peppers to the pot, stirring for 3-4 minutes, or until the shallots become translucent around the edges. Scrape the curry paste into the pot, and stir for 1 minute, allowing the flavors to meld. The contents of the pot should be fragrant and have a red tinge.

2. Once the pumpkin is fragrant, stir in the lime leaves, Thai red chilis, green beans, and coconut milk. When the sauce just begins to boil, lower the heat and maintain a gentle simmer for 20 minutes, stirring at regular intervals to prevent burning. Add the peas after 20 minutes, and stir for an additional 5 minutes.

3. Once the peas have softened, stir in the salt, lime juice, coconut sugar to taste, tamari, and fresh basil leaves.

4. Serve the curry on a bed of hot basmati rice, and garnish with fresh coriander leaves before serving.

# NUTTY LEMON & KALE SALAD

COOK TIME: 0 MINS | MAKES: 6 SERVINGS

## INGREDIENTS:

- 1/4 cup filtered water
- 1 tsp. freshly ground black pepper
- 2 tsp. kosher salt
- 3 tbsp. nutritional yeast
- 3 tsp. crushed garlic
- 4 lemons, juiced, 2 of them zested
- 1/4 cup pure maple syrup
- 1/2 cup raw cashews, soaked and drained
- 1/2 cup extra-virgin avocado oil
- 2 bunches kale, stems removed, leaves sliced crosswise
- 1/2 cup hemp seeds
- 1 cup dried cranberries
- 1 cup toasted almond slivers
- 2 cups cooked quinoa

## DIRECTIONS:

1. In a high-powered food processor, pulse the water, pepper, salt, yeast, garlic, lemon juice, lemon zest, maple syrup, cashews, and avocado oil on high, until you have a lump-free sauce.

2. Place the sliced kale leaves in a large mixing bowl, and scrape half of the dressing from the blender onto the leaves. Stir until all of the leaves are evenly coated. Add the hemp seeds, cranberries, almond slivers, and quinoa, and stir to combine. Add additional dressing if desired, and stir until all of the ingredients are evenly coated in the lemon dressing.

3. Cover, and chill for up to 2 hours, or serve immediately and enjoy!

**Quick Tip:**
Any leftover lemon sauce can be refrigerated in an airtight container for no more than 5 days.

# SWEET & TANGY BAHN MI

COOK TIME: 30 MINS | MAKES: 4 SERVINGS

## INGREDIENTS:

- 1/4 tsp. kosher salt
- 1 tbsp. pure maple syrup
- 1/2 lime, juiced
- 1 tbsp. hot sauce
- 1/2 cup vegan mayonnaise
- 14 oz. extra-firm tofu, pressed, drained, and cubed (½-inch cubes)
- 2 tbsp. rice vinegar
- 2 tbsp. toasted sesame oil
- 2 tbsp. organic dark brown sugar
- 1/4 tsp. flaky sea salt
- 1/4 sweet Vidalia onion, thinly sliced
- 1 English cucumber, thinly sliced
- 1 cup shredded carrots
- 5 oz. baby arugula
- 4 spring onions, thinly sliced (for garnish)
- Fresh coriander leaves, chopped (for garnish)
- 1/4 cup pickled jalapeños, thinly sliced (for garnish)
- 1 lime, quartered (for serving)

## DIRECTIONS:

1. In a small glass bowl, whisk together the kosher salt, maple syrup, lime juice, hot sauce, and mayonnaise, until all of the ingredients are properly combined. Set aside while you prepare the rest of the dish.

2. Set the oven to preheat to 425°F, with the wire rack in the center of the oven, and line a large, rimmed baking sheet with greaseproof paper. Place the tofu cubes, vinegar, oil, sugar, and flaky sea salt in a large bowl, and toss to combine. Spread the seasoned cubes out over the prepared baking sheet in a single layer.

3. Place the sheet in the oven for 30 minutes, flipping the cubes half way through the baking time. They should be nicely browned on all slides. Allow to cool completely on the counter.

4. Divide the onion, cucumber, carrots, and baby arugula between 4 serving bowls. Top each bowl with some toasted tofu cubes. Drizzle the salads with the prepared sauce before garnishing with coriander leaves, jalapeños, and spring onions.

5. Serve the bowls with lime quarters on the side.

# KOREAN VEGGIE BOWLS WITH JACKFRUIT

COOK TIME: 40 MINS | MAKES: 4 SERVINGS

## INGREDIENTS:

**Noodles:**
- 8 oz. Korean glass noodles
- 1 tbsp. toasted sesame oil
- 1 tbsp. organic dark brown sugar
- 1 tbsp. red chili paste
- 1/2 cup tamari

**Vegetables & Jackfruit:**
- 1/2 cup filtered water
- 1 tbsp. red chili paste
- 3 tbsp. organic dark brown sugar
- 1/4 cup tamari
- 1 tbsp. toasted sesame oil
- 2 tbsp. extra-virgin olive oil
- 4 oz. fresh shiitake mushrooms, cleaned, stemmed, and caps thinly sliced
- 1 1/2 lbs. canned young green jackfruit, rinsed and cubed

- 3 tsp. crushed garlic
- 1 tsp. freshly grated ginger
- 2 carrots, julienned
- 1 red bell pepper, stemmed, seeded, and sliced
- 1/2 shallot, thinly sliced
- 4 cups baby spinach leaves
- Kosher salt
- Freshly ground black pepper

**Garnish:**
- 2 tbsp. toasted white sesame seeds
- 0.35 0z. roasted seaweed snack, cut into small strips
- 2 spring onions, thinly sliced
- 1 small cucumber, thinly sliced
- Vegan kimchi
- 1 cup shelled edamame beans, cooked and cooled

## DIRECTIONS:

1. Cook the noodles according to the package instructions, and strain through a colander set over the sink. While the noodles drain, whisk together the toasted sesame oil, dark brown sugar, red chili paste, and tamari in a large mixing bowl. Run the noodles under cold water for one minute, and allow them to drain completely before snipping them into smaller strands with a sharp pair of scissors. Add the noodles to the bowl of sauce, and toss to coat. Set the bowl aside on the counter while you prepare the rest of the dish.

2. In a medium-sized glass bowl, whisk together the filtered water, red chili paste, dark brown sugar, and tamari.

3. In a large frying pan over medium-high heat, heat the sesame oil and 1 tablespoon of olive oil. When the oil is nice and hot, fry the mushrooms for 3-5 minutes until they darken in color.

4. Lower the heat to medium before adding the jackfruit, and stir for 5-8 minutes until the fruit becomes tender. Stir in the garlic and ginger for 30 seconds, or until fragrant. Add the bowl of sauce to the pan, and bring the mixture to a simmer. Lower the heat to maintain a gentle simmer for 10 minutes while stirring. The sauce should thicken and become very syrupy. Once the sauce has thickened and the jackfruit is completely tender, transfer the pan to a wooden chopping board, and set aside.

5. In a separate large frying pan over medium-high heat, heat the remaining olive oil. When it is nice and hot, add the carrots, bell pepper, and shallots, frying for 3-5 minutes, or until the shallots are nicely caramelized and the vegetables are crisp around the edges. Stir in the baby spinach leaves for 30 seconds, or until the leaves begin to wilt. Season the vegetables to taste with salt and pepper.

6. Scrape the bowl of noodles and marinade into the pan with the vegetables, and toss for 1 minute until the noodles are heated through.

7. Divide the noodles and vegetables between 4 serving bowls, and top with the jackfruit.

8. Garnish each bowl with sesame seeds, seaweed snack, spring onions, cucumber, vegan kimchi, and edamame beans. Serve the bowls hot, and enjoy.

# FRESH HERB TABBOULEH

COOK TIME: 15 MINS | MAKES: 4-6 SERVINGS

## INGREDIENTS:

- 3 heirloom tomatoes, cored, and chopped into 1\2-inch pieces
- Kosher salt
- White pepper
- 2 lemons, juiced
- 1/2 cup medium-grain bulgur, rinsed
- 14 oz. extra-firm tofu, cut into 2-inch pieces
- 1/4 cup sunflower oil
- 3 tsp. crushed garlic
- 1/8 tsp. cayenne pepper
- 2 spring onions, thinly sliced
- 1/2 cup fresh mint leaves, chopped
- 1 1/2 cups fresh parsley, minced

## DIRECTIONS:

1. Place the chopped tomatoes in a fine-mesh sieve set over a large bowl, and toss with 1/4 teaspoon of salt. Allow the tomatoes to sit in the sieve for 30 minutes, tossing every few minutes.

2. In a separate large mixing bowl, mix 2 tablespoons of the tomato juice from the bowl beneath the sieve with 2 tablespoons of lemon juice and the bulgur. Allow the bulgur to marinate on the counter for 30-40 minutes, or until the grains have begun to soften.

3. Arrange the tofu on a paper towel-lined baking sheet. You should use 3 or 4 paper towels to absorb the moisture. Press the tofu and allow it to drain for 20 minutes. Add the pressed tofu to a high-powered food processor, and season with a generous pinch of salt and pepper before pulsing the tofu until coarse. Spread the chopped tofu out over a baking sheet with fresh paper towels, and press out any excess moisture.

4. In a large frying pan over medium-high heat, heat 2 teaspoons of sunflower oil. When the oil is nice and hot, fry the drained tofu for 10-12 minutes until nicely browned. Adjust the heat if the tofu is not sizzling after 1 1/2 minutes.

5. Use a wooden spoon to push the browned tofu to the edges of the pan. To the center of the pan, add 1 teaspoon of oil and the garlic. Fry the garlic for 1 minute, or until fragrant. Mix the garlic with the tofu in the pan. Scrape the mixture into a large bowl, and set aside for 10 minutes.

6. In a large mixing bowl, whisk together the remaining lemon juice and oil with 1/2 teaspoon of salt and the cayenne pepper. Stir in the strained tomatoes, softened bulgur, cooked tofu, spring onions, mint, and parsley. Season to taste with salt and pepper. Cover the bowl, and allow the bulgur to soften for 1 additional hour before serving.

# SMOKY BROWN RICE CORN BOWLS

COOK TIME: 45 MINS | MAKES: 4-6 SERVINGS

## INGREDIENTS:

- Kosher salt
- 1 1/2 cups uncooked, long grain brown rice, rinsed
- White pepper
- 1 1/2 tsp. ground cilantro seeds
- 1 1/2 tsp. ground cumin
- 1 tbsp. freshly squeezed lime juice
- 5 tbsp. extra-virgin olive oil
- 2 corn ears, kernels cut from the cob

- 3 tsp. crushed garlic
- 3 poblano peppers, cored, seeded, and chopped (1/2-inch pieces)
- 1 shallot, chopped
- 1/4 cup filtered water
- 15 oz. canned black turtle beans, rinsed
- 1/2 cup store-bought chipotle sauce
- 1/4 cup fresh coriander leaves, chopped (for garnish)

## DIRECTIONS:

1. In a large pot over high heat, bring 4 quarts of water to a rolling boil. Add 1 tablespoon of salt to the pot, along with the uncooked rice. Stir, and bring the pot back up to a boil. Cook the rice for 25-30 minutes, stirring at regular intervals until it is cooked. Strain the rice.

2. In a large mixing bowl, whisk together 1/4 teaspoon salt, 1/4 teaspoon pepper, 1/2 teaspoon cilantro seeds, 1/2 teaspoon cumin, the lime juice, and 2 tablespoons oil. Add the strained rice, and stir with a wooden spoon. Cover the bowl and set aside.

3. In a large frying pan over medium-high heat, heat 1 tablespoon of oil. When the oil is nice and hot, fry the corn kernels with 1/4 teaspoon each of salt and pepper for 3 minutes, or until the corn begins to brown. Scrape into a clean mixing bowl, and cover.

4. In the same frying pan, heat 1 tablespoon of oil. When the oil is hot, fry 2 teaspoons of garlic, along with the remaining cilantro seeds and cumin, for 30 seconds, or until fragrant. Add the peppers to the pan, and fry while stirring for an additional 6-8 minutes. Scrape the mixture into a third mixing bowl, and cover.

5. In the same skillet over medium heat, heat the remaining tablespoon of oil. Add the shallots, and fry for 5-7 minutes, or until they begin to caramelize. Add the remaining garlic, and allow the flavors to meld for 30 seconds. Stir in the filtered water and black turtle beans until the sauce begins to simmer. Lower the heat to maintain a gentle simmer for about 2 minutes while stirring, or until the beans are heated through and the sauce has thickened.

6. Scoop the rice into 5 serving bowls and top with the peppers, followed by the cooked corn and hot beans. Spoon the chipotle sauce onto each bowl, and garnish with fresh coriander leaves before serving.

# WRAPS, SANDWICHES, & BURGERS

# RUSSIAN-DRESSED REUBEN BURGERS

COOK TIME: 15-20 MINS | MAKES: 2 SERVINGS

## INGREDIENTS:

- 1 tsp. crushed ginger
- 2 tbsp. ketchup
- 1/4 cup vegan mayonnaise
- 2 vegan burger patties
- 1/2 cup sauerkraut
- 2 slices vegan cheese
- 1 tbsp. filtered water
- 2 vegan-friendly burger buns
- 2 large dill pickles

## DIRECTIONS:

1. In a small mixing bowl, whisk together the ginger, ketchup, and mayonnaise. Set the bowl aside on the counter while you prepare the rest of the dish.

2. In a large frying pan with a fitted lid, prepare the vegan patties according to package instructions. When they are cooked, spoon the sauerkraut onto each patty, and cover with a slice of vegan cheese. Carefully add the water to the pan. Place the fitted lid on the pan, and allow the patties to steam until the cheese has melted – about 1 minute.

3. Place the cooked patties on the buns, and dollop each burger with the Russian dressing. Serve the burgers with pickles on the side, and enjoy!

# TAHINI-DRESSED SMOKY CHICKPEA WRAPS

COOK TIME: 10 MINS | MAKES: 4 SERVINGS

## INGREDIENTS:

**Dressing:**
- 2 tsp. crushed garlic
- 1 tsp. tamari
- 1 tbsp. extra-virgin olive oil
- 1 tbsp. rice vinegar
- 1 1/2 tbsp. freshly squeezed lemon juice
- 3 tbsp. warm filtered water
- 1/4 cup tahini sauce

**Chickpeas:**
- 1 tbsp. extra virgin olive oil
- 30 oz. canned chickpeas, rinsed and drained
- 1 tsp. tamari

- 1 tsp. pure maple syrup
- 2 tbsp. freshly squeezed lemon juice
- 1/2 tsp. red pepper flakes
- 1 tsp. garlic powder
- 2 tsp. ground cumin
- 2 tsp. sweet smoked paprika

**Serving:**
- 4 large corn wraps
- Carrot sticks
- Cucumber sticks
- Baby spinach

## DIRECTIONS:

1. In a small glass bowl, whisk together the crushed garlic, tamari, olive oil, rice vinegar, lemon juice, warm filtered water, and tahini sauce. Set the bowl aside on the counter while you prepare the rest of the dish.

2. In a large frying pan over medium-high heat, heat the olive oil. When the oil is nice and hot, fry the chickpeas for 3-5 minutes, or until they turn a crispy golden brown. In a clean glass bowl, whisk together the tamari, maple syrup, and lemon juice. When the chickpeas are toasted and browned, add the sauce mixture, and stir for 30 seconds until the liquid reduces.

3. Stir in the red pepper flakes, garlic powder, cumin, and sweet smoked paprika, allowing the flavors to meld for an additional 30 seconds. Transfer the pan to a wooden chopping board.

4. Spoon the cooked chickpeas onto the wraps, and add the vegetables as desired.

5. Spoon the tahini sauce over the wraps, and serve.

# HEARTY MISO MUSHROOM PATTIES

COOK TIME: 30 MINS | MAKES: 4 SERVINGS

## INGREDIENTS:

- 1 tbsp. extra-virgin olive oil
- 4 tsp. crushed garlic
- 1 small shallot, diced
- 1 lb. button mushrooms, sliced
- 1 tbsp. tamari
- Kosher salt
- 1/8 tsp. white pepper
- 3 tbsp. white miso paste
- 1 1/2 cups cooked brown rice
- 1 tsp. toasted sesame seeds
- 1/4 cup all-purpose flour (more if needed)
- 2/3 cup panko breadcrumbs
- Sunflower oil

**Spicy Mayo:**
- 1 tsp. toasted sesame seeds
- 1 tbsp. hot sauce
- 3 tbsp. vegan mayonnaise

**Burgers:**
- Sliced onions
- Sliced tomatoes
- Iceberg lettuce
- 4 vegan buns

## DIRECTIONS:

1. In a large frying pan over medium-high heat, heat the oil. When the oil is nice and hot, fry the garlic and shallots for 2 minutes, allowing the flavors to meld. Turn the heat up to high, and stir in the mushrooms. Add the tamari, and salt to taste. Fry the mushrooms for 3 minutes while stirring, or until they begin to darken in color. Turn off the heat, and leave the mushrooms in the pan for 5 minutes.

2. Scrape the cooked mushrooms into a blender, along with the pepper, miso paste, and cooked brown rice. Pulse the mixture 3-4 times, or until the rice and mushrooms are properly incorporated. You don't want the mixture to be too fine, so leave a few large pieces of mushroom. Scape the contents of the blender into a large mixing bowl, and add the sesame seeds, flour, and breadcrumbs. Use a wooden spoon to properly combine the mixture. Taste, and add more salt if needed.

3. Use clean hands to work with the mixture. Press a generous portion of the mixture into a ball. If the mixture does not hold its shape, add 1-2 tablespoons of flour to the bowl, and combine. When the mixture is able to hold its shape, divide it into 4 balls of roughly the same size, and press them down into 1-inch-thick patties.

4. In the same pan you used to fry the patties, heat enough sunflower oil to coat the bottom. When the oil is nice and hot, fry the patties for 10 minutes, flipping half way through the cooking time. The patties should be cooked all the way through, with both sides nicely browned. Transfer to a plate, and tent to keep warm.

5. To make the spicy mayonnaise: In a small glass bowl, whisk together the sesame seeds, hot sauce, and mayonnaise.

6. Serve the patties as is with spicy mayonnaise and toppings, or add vegan buns and build some burgers!

# SWEET & SMOKY TOFU SANDWICHES

COOK TIME: 30 MINS | MAKES: 4 SERVINGS

## INGREDIENTS:

- 1/2 tsp. kosher salt
- 1/4 tsp. white pepper
- 2 tsp. onion powder
- 2 tsp. garlic powder
- 1 tsp. sweet smoked paprika
- 1/4 cup organic dark brown sugar
- 1 tbsp. French mustard
- 2 tbsp. tamari
- 2 tbsp. extra-virgin olive oil
- 14 oz. extra-firm tofu, cut into 8 slices
- 2 pinches flaky sea salt
- 1/2 tsp. balsamic vinegar
- 1/4 cup vegan mayonnaise
- 1 cup red cabbage, shredded
- 1/2 cup canned pineapple chunks, drained
- 4 ciabatta rolls

## DIRECTIONS:

1. Set the oven to preheat to 425°F, with the wire rack in the center of the oven, and line a large, rimmed baking sheet with greaseproof paper.

2. In a large mixing bowl, whisk together the salt, pepper, onion powder, garlic powder, paprika, brown sugar, mustard, tamari, and olive oil. Arrange the tofu slices on the prepared baking sheet in a single layer. Use a basting brush to coat the tops of the tofu slices with half of the sauce. Bake the tofu in the oven for 15 minutes. Remove the sheet from the oven, and use a spatula to carefully flip the tofu slices. Coat the other side of the tofu with the sauce, and return the sheet to the oven for an additional 15 minutes. The tofu should be golden brown when done.

3. Meanwhile, in a large mixing bowl, use a wooden spoon to combine the flaky sea salt, balsamic vinegar, mayonnaise, cabbage, and pineapple chunks.

4. Slice the ciabatta rolls in half, and fill each roll with 2 slices of roasted tofu and a generous helping of pineapple slaw.

# NUTTY SMOKED CHICKPEA SALAD SANDWICHES

COOK TIME: 10 MINS | MAKES: 4-6 SERVINGS

## INGREDIENTS:

- 1 tsp. pure maple syrup
- 1 tsp. tamari
- 1/2 tsp. extra-virgin olive oil
- 2 1/2 tsp. liquid smoke
- 1 tsp. garlic powder
- 1 tsp. sweet smoked paprika
- 2 tsp. nutritional yeast
- 3/4 cup raw almond slivers
- 3 tbsp. freshly squeezed lemon juice
- 1 Hass avocado, peeled, pitted, and chopped
- 3 cups canned chickpeas, rinsed and drained
- 1-2 tsp. sriracha sauce
- 1/2 tsp. flaky sea salt
- White pepper to taste
- 1/3 cup celery, chopped
- 1/3 cup fresh dill, chopped
- 1/2 medium red onion, chopped
- Vegan bread
- French mustard
- Heirloom tomatoes
- Iceberg lettuce

## DIRECTIONS:

1. Set the oven to preheat to 350°F, with the wire rack in the center of the oven, and lightly spray a baking sheet with baking spray.

2. In a small glass bowl, whisk together the maple syrup, tamari, olive oil, and liquid smoke. In a separate glass bowl, whisk together the garlic powder, sweet smoked paprika, and nutritional yeast. Add the almond slivers to the bowl of sauce, and stir for one minute. Use a slotted spoon to transfer the almonds to the bowl of spices, and stir to combine until all of the slivers are evenly coated. Fan the almond slivers out on the prepared baking sheet, and roast in the oven for 10 minutes, flipping half way through the baking time. Allow the almonds to cool completely on the baking sheet.

3. In a large mixing bowl, use a fork to mash the lemon juice, avocado, and chickpeas together, leaving a few chunks, if desired, for texture. Use a rubber spatula to fold in the sriracha, flaky sea salt, pepper, celery, dill, and red onion. Add the almond slivers to the bowl, and stir to combine.

4. Spoon the filling onto vegan bread, and top with French mustard, tomatoes, and lettuce before serving.

**Quick Tip:**
This salad filling is best eaten in one sitting, as it tends to lose its crunch when refrigerated overnight.

# SMOKED CARROT & TOFU ROLLS

COOK TIME: 20 MINS | MAKES: 4 SERVINGS

## INGREDIENTS:

- 1/2 tsp. ground cumin
- 4 tsp. crushed garlic
- 2 tsp. pure maple syrup
- 1 1/2 tbsp. liquid smoke
- 2 tbsp. freshly squeezed lemon juice
- 1/4 cup tamari
- 1 cup vegetable stock
- 2 medium carrots, sliced into 1/2-inch thick strips, 2 inches long
- 8 oz. tofu, sliced into 1/2-inch thick strips, 2 inches long
- 1 tbsp. extra-virgin avocado oil
- 4 ciabatta rolls, lightly toasted
- French mustard
- Iceberg lettuce
- 1-2 heirloom tomatoes, sliced
- 1/2 red onion, sliced
- 1 Hass avocado, peeled, pitted, and sliced

## DIRECTIONS:

1. In a medium-sized pot over medium-low heat, whisk together the cumin, garlic, maple syrup, liquid smoke, lemon juice, tamari, and vegetable stock.

2. Once the stock begins to simmer, add the carrot and tofu sticks, stirring for 30 seconds and allowing the flavors to meld. Turn off the heat, and pour the mixture into a shallow casserole dish in a single layer. Cover the dish, and chill for 4-8 hours.

3. Once the carrots and tofu have marinated, heat the avocado oil in a large frying pan over medium heat. When the oil is nice and hot, fry the carrots and tofu for 2-3 minutes per side, or until the tofu is golden and the carrots are crispy and fork-tender. Keep an eye on the carrots, as they tend to cook much quicker than the tofu. Add a few tablespoons of the marinade if the liquid in the pan is evaporating too quickly. Transfer the cooked tofu and carrots to a plate, and tent to keep warm.

4. To assemble the rolls, slice the lightly toasted rolls in half, and spread the cut sides with mustard as desired. Fill the rolls with cooked carrots, cooked tofu, lettuce, tomato, onions, and avocado slices. Serve immediately, and enjoy.

# VEGAN SAN CHOY BOW

COOK TIME: 20 MINS | MAKES: 8 SERVINGS

## INGREDIENTS:

**Filling:**
- 14 oz. extra-firm tempeh
- 1 tbsp. extra-virgin olive oil
- 1/2 tsp. fresh ginger, grated
- 1 tsp. crushed garlic
- 1 small shallot, diced
- 1 small carrot, diced
- 6 fresh shiitake mushrooms, cubed (1/4-inch thick)
- 2 tbsp. dry sherry

**Sauce:**
- 1/2 tsp. kikkoman soy sauce
- 1 tsp. organic dark brown sugar
- 2 tbsp. filtered water, room temperature
- 1 1/2 tbsp. hoisin sauce

- 1 tsp. toasted sesame oil
- 1 tbsp. vegan oyster sauce
- 1 1/2 tsp. corn flour

**Bonus Sweet Sauce (optional):**
- 1/2 tsp. corn flour
- 1 1/2 tsp. dark brown sugar, or to taste
- 3 tbsp. filtered water
- 1 tbsp. hoisin sauce

**Serving:**
- 8 large lettuce leaves
- Bird's eye chili, chopped
- Spring onions, chopped
- 2 tbsp. crushed peanuts

## DIRECTIONS:

1. Place the tempeh between 2 stacks of kitchen towels on a clean baking sheet – 4 towels on top and 4 underneath. Place a heavy pot or stack of books on top of the tempeh, and leave for 10 minutes to drain any excess water. Once the tempeh has been pressed, slice it into cubes and crumble them into a large mixing bowl. Set aside.

2. In a small glass bowl, whisk together the soy sauce, dark brown sugar, filtered water, hoisin sauce, toasted sesame oil, vegan oyster sauce, and corn flour. Set the bowl aside while you prepare the rest of the dish.

3. In a large wok over medium heat, heat the olive oil. Once the oil is nice and hot, fry the ginger, garlic, and shallots for 2 minutes, allowing the flavors to meld. Once the mixture is fragrant, toss in the carrots and mushrooms. Raise the heat to high, and stir in the sherry, then gently stir the filling for 2-3 minutes until the carrots are fork-tender.

4. Reduce the heat to medium-high and stir in the crumbled tempeh, along with the soy and corn flour sauce mixture. Fry for 1o minutes, gently tossing every 2 minutes, until the tempeh is lightly toasted and most of the liquid has evaporated. Taste, and adjust the seasoning as desired.

5. Scrape the mixture into a serving bowl, and allow to cool for 10 minutes.

6. If making the sweet sauce: In a small pot over medium heat, whisk together the corn flour, organic dark brown sugar to taste, water, and hoisin sauce. You may want to add the sugar a little at a time and adjust to your liking, as hoisin sauce is naturally sweet. Simmer for 2 minutes, or until the sauce thickens. Transfer the pot to a wooden chopping board.

7. Divide the 8 lettuce leaves between 8 bowls or plates, and top each leaf with the filling. Garnish the filling with chili, spring onions, and crushed peanuts before drizzling with the sweet sauce if desired. Serve, and enjoy the delicate, sweet taste.

# CREAMY VEGAN MEDITERRANEAN BURGER

COOK TIME: 15 MINS | MAKES: 2 SERVINGS

## INGREDIENTS:

- 2 vegan burger patties
- 1/4 cup pimento olives, sliced
- 2 slices vegan mozzarella cheese
- 1 tbsp. filtered water
- 2 lightly toasted ciabatta buns
- 2 tbsp. vegan mayonnaise
- 1 heirloom tomato, sliced
- 1/4 cup iceberg lettuce, grated

## DIRECTIONS:

1. In a large frying pan, prepare the burger patties according to package instructions. When the burgers are cooked, divide the pimento olives in half, and top each patty with olives and a slice of vegan cheese. Add the filtered water to the pan around the patties, and cover with a fitted lid. Allow the cheese to melt for 45-60 seconds in the covered pan.

2. Slice the ciabatta buns in half, and slather the bottom halves with vegan mayonnaise – 1 tablespoon per bun. Build the buns with tomato slices and shredded lettuce before topping with the patties.

3. Serve the burgers hot, and enjoy.

# HEARTY MUSHROOM & SPROUTS WRAPS

COOK TIME: 30 MINS | MAKES: 2 SERVINGS

## INGREDIENTS:

- 1/2 cup canned chickpeas, rinsed and drained
- 1 1/2 cups Brussels sprouts, trimmed and roughly chopped
- 5 oz. sliced shiitake mushrooms
- 2 tbsp. extra-virgin avocado oil
- 1/2 tsp. Himalayan salt
- 1/2 tsp. freshly ground black pepper
- 1/2 red onion, thinly sliced
- 2 tsp. pure maple syrup
- 2 large flour or corn wraps
- Vegan sour cream
- Hot sauce

## DIRECTIONS:

1. Line a large baking tray with greaseproof paper, and set the oven to preheat to 400°F, with the wire rack in the center of the oven.

2. In a large mixing bowl, toss the chickpeas, Brussels sprouts, and mushrooms with half of the oil and the salt and pepper, until all of the ingredients are evenly coated in the spices. Fan the mixture out in a single layer on half of the prepared baking tray. Add the onions to the same bowl, and toss with the remaining oil. Fan the onions out on the other half of the tray in a single layer.

3. Bake in the oven for 15 minutes, then use a spatula to flip everything on the tray. Drizzle the onions with the pure maple syrup before placing the tray in the oven for an additional 15 minutes.

4. Remove the tray from the oven, and toss the ingredients to combine. Spoon the filling into the wraps in equal amounts, and top with sour cream and hot sauce. Fold the edges of each wrap inwards, and roll up before serving.

**Quick Tip:**
The tighter you roll the wraps, the less mess you will create when eating. If you are unsure, look up a tutorial online on how to correctly fold a burrito or wrap.

# FAN-FAVORITE BROCCOLI BURRITOS

COOK TIME: 35 MINS | MAKES: 4-6 SERVINGS

## INGREDIENTS:

- 15 oz. canned chickpeas, rinsed and drained
- 1 large crown broccoli
- 1 red bell pepper
- 1 shallot
- 1-2 tbsp. tamari
- 3 tbsp. extra-virgin olive oil
- Red pepper flakes to taste
- 1/2 tsp. ground cilantro seeds
- 1 tsp. sweet smoked paprika
- 1 tsp. ground cumin
- 2 tsp. chili powder
- 4 tsp. crushed garlic
- 1/2 lime, juiced
- 4-6 corn or flour wraps
- Fresh coriander leaves, chopped
- Avocado, peeled, pitted, and sliced
- Spinach, stemmed and chopped

## DIRECTIONS:

1. Set the oven to preheat to 425°F, with the wire rack in the center of the oven.

2. Place the chickpeas in a large mixing bowl. Chop the broccoli, bell pepper, and shallot into small pieces, roughly the same size as the chickpeas. Add the chopped vegetables to the bowl of chickpeas, and sprinkle with the tamari and olive oil. Toss to coat.

3. In a small glass bowl, whisk together the red pepper flakes, ground cilantro seeds, paprika, cumin, and chili powder. Sprinkle the spice mixture over the coated vegetables, and toss until everything is evenly coated with the spice mixture. Fan the vegetables out in an even layer on a large, rimmed baking sheet. Place the sheet in the oven for 20 minutes.

4. Remove the sheet from the oven, and toss the vegetables with the crushed garlic. Return the sheet to the oven for an additional 15 minutes. The broccoli may appear charred at this point, but don't panic, a little charring around the edges is preferable.

5. Remove the tray from the oven, and toss the vegetables with the lime juice. Taste, and adjust the seasoning as desired.

6. Divide the roasted vegetables between the wraps, and top with coriander leaves, avocado, and spinach. Fold the wraps like burritos, and serve.

# RED LENTIL & NAVY BEAN PATTIES

COOK TIME: 40 MINS | MAKES: 8 SERVINGS

## INGREDIENTS:

- 2/3 cup filtered water
- 1/3 cup red lentils
- 15 oz. canned navy beans, drained
- 1/2 lime, zested
- 1/2 tsp. flaky sea salt
- 1/4 tsp. white pepper
- 1 tsp. extra-virgin olive oil
- 1 tsp. ground cumin
- 1 1/2 tsp. all-purpose, no-salt-added seasoning blend
- 1 1/2 tsp. sweet smoked paprika
- 1/2 cup panko bread crumbs (more if needed)
- 1 jalapeño, minced
- 3 tsp. crushed garlic
- 1/2 shallot, finely chopped
- Vegan-friendly baking spray

## DIRECTIONS:

1. In a large pot over medium heat, bring the filtered water to a rolling boil. Once the water is boiling, add the lentils. When the water comes to a simmer again, lower the heat to maintain a gentle simmer for about 10 minutes, or until the lentils are completely soft. Strain the lentils, and allow them to cool while you prepare the rest of the dish.

2. Place the navy beans in a large mixing bowl, and add the cooled lentils. Mash the beans and lentils with a fork. Add the lime zest, sea salt, white pepper, olive oil, cumin, all-purpose seasoning, paprika, bread crumbs, jalapeño, garlic, and shallots. Use a wooden spoon to stir and thoroughly combine the ingredients. Using clean hands, form a portion of the mixture into a small ball. If the ball does not maintain its shape, add bread crumbs as needed.

3. Spray a large, rimmed baking sheet with baking spray. Divide the mixture into 8 balls of roughly the same size, and arrange them on the prepared baking sheet before pressing them into patties about 1-inch thick. Chill for a minimum of 30 minutes, or up to 4 hours.

4. Set the oven to preheat to 400°F, with the wire rack in the center of the oven.

5. When the burgers are properly chilled, coat them with baking spray before placing the sheet in the oven for 15 minutes. Flip the patties, and bake for an additional 15 minutes, or until they are nicely browned on both sides.

6. Serve the patties as is, with sides of your choice, or get creative and build some burgers with ciabatta buns.

# FLAVOR-FILLED PORTOBELLO BURGERS

COOK TIME: 15 MINS | MAKES: 4 SERVINGS

## INGREDIENTS:

- Flaky sea salt
- White pepper
- 1 tsp. crushed garlic
- 3 tbsp. red wine vinegar
- 1/2 cup extra-virgin avocado oil
- 4 large Portobello mushrooms
- 1/2 cup sun-dried tomatoes, patted dry and chopped
- 1/2 cup jarred roasted red peppers, patted dry and chopped
- 1/4 cup fresh basil leaves, chopped
- 1/4 cup vegan mayonnaise
- 1 medium red onion sliced into (1/2-inch thick) rounds
- 4 ciabatta buns, sliced in half
- 1 cup baby arugula

## DIRECTIONS:

1. In a shallow casserole dish, whisk together 1 teaspoon salt, 1/2 teaspoon pepper, the garlic, red wine vinegar, and avocado oil. Place the mushrooms on a wooden chopping board, and remove the stems and gills. Rinse the mushrooms, and allow them to drain. Use a sharp knife to score the mushroom caps on the outside, taking care not to slice all the way through. You only need a few shallow slits.

2. Submerge the caps in the bowl of marinade, and cover. Allow the mushrooms to marinate for a minimum of 30 minutes, or 1 hour.

3. In a large mixing bowl, toss together the sun-dried tomatoes and roasted red peppers. In a second mixing bowl, whisk together the basil leaves and mayonnaise.

4. Set the grill to preheat on high. Transfer the mushrooms to a plate, and add the onion rounds to the bowl of marinade.

5. When the grill is nice and hot, lower the temperature to medium-high and grill the mushrooms and onions for 4-6 minutes. Flip, and grill the other sides for 3-5 minutes. The mushrooms should darken in color.

6. Transfer the onions and mushrooms to a plate. Place the mushrooms hollow side up, and spoon the tomato and pepper mixture into them. Use the back of a spoon to gently press the mixture into the caps.

7. Place the sliced buns on the hot grill, and toast for 1 minute per side.

8. Build the burgers by spreading the basil mayonnaise over the cut side of each bun. Place 1 mushroom cap and 1 onion ring on the bottom half of each bun, and top with baby arugula. Close the buns, and serve.

# SWEET & STICKY BBQ WRAPS

COOK TIME: 40-60 MINS | MAKES: 4 SERVINGS

## INGREDIENTS:

- 1 1/2 tsp. corn flour
- 1 1/2 tsp. hot sauce
- 1 1/2 tbsp. rice vinegar
- 5 tsp. crushed garlic
- 6 tbsp. filtered water
- 6 tbsp. kikkoman soy sauce
- 3/4 cup organic dark brown sugar
- 1/4 cup extra-virgin olive oil
- 1 lb. extra-firm tofu, sliced into 1/2-inch strips
- 4 large flour or corn wraps
- 3 radishes, trimmed, halved, and thinly sliced
- 1 cup fresh coriander leaves, chopped
- 8 oz. baby Bok choy, thinly sliced, crosswise
- 2 spring onions, thinly chopped

## DIRECTIONS:

1. In a small glass bowl, whisk together the corn flour, hot sauce, rice vinegar, garlic, water, soy sauce, and dark brown sugar. Set the bowl aside on the counter.

2. In a large frying pan over medium heat, heat 2 tablespoons of olive oil. When the oil is nice and hot, fry half of the tofu for 2-4 minutes per side, or until browned evenly on all sides. Use a slotted spoon to transfer the cooked tofu to a paper towel-lined bowl, and repeat the process with 2 tablespoons of oil and the rest of the tofu.

3. In the same pan over medium-low heat, stir the sauce mixture from the glass bowl for about 5 minutes, or until the sauce thickens and reduces to about 1 cup. Turn off the heat.

4. Discard the paper towels from the bowl of tofu, and add half of the sauce. Toss until all of the tofu strips are evenly coated in sauce.

5. Lay the wraps on a clean counter. Divide the tofu strips between the wraps, and top with radishes, coriander leaves, baby Bok choy, and spring onions. Drizzle each wrap with 1 tablespoon of sauce, and tightly fold and roll the edges like a burrito.

6. Serve the folded wraps with the extra sauce on the side.

# MAIN MEALS

# CREAMY HERB & CAULIFLOWER PASTA

COOK TIME: 30 MINS | MAKES: 4 SERVINGS

## INGREDIENTS:

- 1 lb. rotini pasta
- 4 cups kale
- Pinch of salt
- 1 lb. cauliflower florets
- 1 tsp. miso paste
- 1 tbsp. extra-virgin olive oil
- 1 tbsp. freshly squeezed lemon juice
- 2-3 tsp. crushed garlic
- 1/2 cup unsweetened soy milk
- 1/8 teaspoon of salt
- White pepper
- 1/3 cup fresh parsley, chopped

## DIRECTIONS:

1. Cook the pasta by following the package instructions, then drain. In a large mixing bowl, toss the pasta with the kale, and set the bowl aside.

2. Bring a large pot of filtered water to a rolling boil over medium heat. When the water is boiling, add a small amount of salt and the cauliflower florets. Boil the florets for 5-7 minutes, or until they are fork-tender. Pour the cauliflower into a strainer set over the sink.

3. Place the drained cauliflower in a high-powered food processor, along with the miso paste, olive oil, lemon juice, garlic, soy milk, and 1/8 teaspoon of salt. Pulse the food processor until you have a smooth sauce. Taste, and adjust the seasoning as desired.

4. Scrape the sauce into a large pot placed over low heat, and add the kale and pasta. Stir the pasta for a few minutes, until everything is heated through. Scrape the pasta into a serving bowl, and season with salt and pepper as desired. Garnish with fresh parsley, and serve straight away.

# SWEET & TANGY THAI FRIED RICE

COOK TIME: 20 MINS | MAKES: 3 SERVINGS

## INGREDIENTS:

- 3 tbsp. extra-virgin olive oil
- 14 oz. extra-firm tempeh, pressed and sliced (1/2-inch cubes)
- 1/2 tsp. kosher salt (divided)
- 1/2 cup red bell pepper, seeded and diced
- 1 small shallot, diced
- 3 cups cooked rice, cooled
- 1/4 tsp. white pepper
- 1/2 tsp. cayenne pepper
- 2 tsp. curry powder
- 2 tsp. organic dark brown sugar
- 2 tsp. kikkoman soy sauce
- 1 cup canned pineapple pieces (1/2-inch chunks)
- 1/2 cup heirloom tomatoes, seeded and diced
- 1/2 cup spring onions, diced (extra for garnish)
- 1/3 cup roasted cashews

## DIRECTIONS:

1. Heat the oil in a large wok over medium-high heat. When the oil is nice and hot, add the tempeh cubes with 1/4 teaspoon salt. Fry the tempeh for ten minutes, until all sides are nicely toasted. The cubes should be tossed every 2 minutes to prevent burning.

2. Add the peppers and shallots, stirring for 2 minutes, or until the peppers are tender. Add the rice, and toss to combine. Add the remaining salt, the white pepper, cayenne pepper, curry powder, brown sugar, and soy sauce. Toss until all of the ingredients are properly combined.

3. Stir in the pineapple chunks, and raise the heat to high. Fry for 2-3 minutes until the pineapple is heated through, tossing regularly. Add the tomatoes, cashews, and spring onions, and fry for an additional 2 minutes. Turn off the heat and taste the rice. Adjust the seasoning as desired.

4. Divide the fried rice between 3 bowls, and serve hot, garnished with extra spring onions.

# HEARTY MUSHROOM & WINE POLENTA

COOK TIME: 60 MINS | MAKES: 4 SERVINGS

## INGREDIENTS:

- 1 lb. button mushrooms, quartered
- 3 1/2 cups baby tomatoes
- 8 fresh thyme sprigs
- 3 tsp. crushed garlic
- 1 1/2 tsp. Himalayan salt
- 1/4 tsp. ground white pepper
- 4 tbsp. extra-virgin avocado oil
- 1/2 cup dry white wine, vegan
- 4 cups filtered water
- 1 cup cornmeal
- 1 tbsp. nutritional yeast

## DIRECTIONS:

1. Set the oven to preheat to 425°F, with the wire rack in the center of the oven.

In a large mixing bowl, toss together the mushrooms, baby tomatoes, thyme sprigs, garlic, 1/2 teaspoon salt, pepper, and 3 tablespoons of oil, until all of the mushrooms and tomatoes are evenly coated. Fan the seasoned vegetables out on a large, rimmed baking sheet in an even layer, and bake in the oven for 25-30 minutes, or until the mushrooms darken in color and the tomatoes begin to release their juices.

Remove the sheet from the oven, and pour the wine over everything on the sheet. Return to the oven for 2-3 minutes, or until the sauce is bubbling. Allow to cool slightly on the counter.

In a medium-sized pot over medium-high heat, bring the filtered water to a rolling boil. Once the water is boiling, gradually whisk in the uncooked polenta, and lower the heat to maintain a gentle simmer for 25-30 minutes. Stir the pot at regular intervals to prevent burning, until the polenta is soft and creamy. Add the remaining salt and oil, stirring to combine.

Divide the cooked polenta into 4 bowls, and serve hot with the mushrooms and tomatoes spooned over the top.

# ZESTY CITRUS SEITAN

COOK TIME: 15-20 MINS | MAKES: 4 SERVINGS

## INGREDIENTS:

**Citrus Sauce:**
- 1 tbsp. corn flour
- 4 tsp. cold filtered water
- 1/8 tsp. red pepper flakes
- 3/4 tsp. fresh ginger, grated
- 1/2 cup freshly squeezed orange juice
- 1 tsp. finely grated orange zest
- 2 tsp. crushed garlic
- 3 tbsp. kikkoman soy sauce
- 3 tbsp. distilled white vinegar
- 1/4 cup organic dark brown sugar
- 1/2 cup vegetable stock

- 6 orange peel strips
- 6 dried bird's eye chilis
- 1 spring onion, thinly sliced
- Himalayan salt

**Seitan:**
- 1/2 cup cornmeal
- 1 1/2 cups corn flour
- 1 cup full-fat coconut milk
- 1 lb. seitan, drained and patted dry, sliced into 1-inch pieces
- 3 cups sunflower oil

## DIRECTIONS:

1. In a small glass bowl, whisk together the corn flour and cold water. Set aside.

2. In a large pot over high heat, whisk together the red pepper flakes, ginger, orange juice, orange zest, garlic, soy sauce, distilled vinegar, sugar, and vegetable stock. When the stock begins to boil, gradually whisk in the corn flour and water mixture. Reduce the heat to medium-low, and allow the sauce to simmer for 1 minute, or until the sauce has thickened slightly. Remove the pot from the heat, and tent to keep warm.

3. Set the oven to preheat to 200°F, with the wire rack in the center of the oven. Line a large, rimmed baking sheet with greaseproof paper, and place the sheet on the center rack while the oven preheats.

4. In a large casserole dish, whisk together the cornmeal and corn flour. Place the coconut milk in a large mixing bowl, and lay the seitan slices in the milk. Gently lift the pieces of seitan, and allow the excess milk to drip off. Dredge the seitan pieces in the flour mixture, gently pressing them down so that the flour sticks to them. Lay the coated slices on a clean plate, and repeat with all of the seitan pieces.

5. Heat the oil in a large frying pan over medium-high heat. When the oil is nice and hot, fry half of the seitan slices, using a spatula to flip them now and then, for about 7-11 minutes. The slices should be golden brown. Use a spatula to transfer the seitan to the prepared sheet in the oven. Repeat with the remaining coated seitan slices.

6. Add the orange peel strips and chilis to the pot of sauce, and whisk before stirring in the seitan. Season to taste with salt, and serve garnished with the sliced spring onions.

# SMOKY YAMS & BLACK-EYED PEAS

COOK TIME: 1-2 HOURS | MAKES: 6 SERVINGS

## INGREDIENTS:

- 1 1/2 cups dried black-eyed peas
- 3 medium to large yams
- 2 tbsp. extra-virgin olive oil
- 1 shallot, diced
- 3 celery stalks, finely chopped
- 1/2 tsp. sweet smoked paprika
- 1/2 tsp. ground nutmeg
- 1/2 tsp. ground allspice
- 1/4 tsp. kosher salt
- 3-4 chipotle peppers in adobo sauce, chopped into pea-size pieces
- 2-3 tsp. crushed garlic
- 3 cups vegetable stock
- 2-3 bunches steamed kale

## DIRECTIONS:

1. Rinse the black-eyed peas with fresh water, and discard any bad ones. Place the rinsed peas in a large mixing bowl, and cover with filtered water. Allow the peas to soak for at least 6 hours or overnight.

2. Set the oven to preheat to 400°F, with the wire rack in the center of the oven.

3. Place the yams on a large, rimmed baking sheet, and use a fork to poke the skins all over. Bake the yams in the oven for 45 minutes, or until they are fork-tender.

4. In a large pot over medium heat, heat the olive oil. When the oil is nice and hot, fry the shallots for about 5 minutes, or until the edges begin to caramelize. Stir in the celery and fry for 2 minutes, or until the pieces begin to soften. Add the paprika, nutmeg, allspice, and salt, allowing the flavors to meld for 30 seconds. Add the chipotle peppers and garlic to taste, and stir for an additional 30 seconds.

5. Stir in the stock and soaked peas, and bring to a simmer. Adjust the heat to maintain a gentle simmer for 30-60 minutes, or until the peas are completely soft. Cooking time may vary depending on the peas. Add more stock or water as needed, or simply drain the excess stock if the peas cook quickly. Once the peas are done, taste, and adjust the seasoning as desired.

6. When the yams are done, slice them in half lengthwise, and place each half on a serving plate. Use a fork to fluff the inside of the yams, and season as desired. Top each yam with 1 cup of peas and 2 cups of kale. Serve hot, and enjoy.

# GINGER & GARLIC BROCCOLI STIR-FRY

COOK TIME: 30 MINS | MAKES: 4 SERVINGS

## INGREDIENTS:

- 14 oz. extra-firm tempeh
- 1 1/2 tsp. corn flour
- 1/4 cup vegetable stock
- 1 tbsp. organic dark brown sugar
- 3 tbsp. kikkoman soy sauce
- Sunflower oil
- 1 spring onion, chopped
- 6 tsp. crushed garlic
- 1 tsp. freshly grated ginger
- 1/4 cup filtered water or more vegetable stock
- Himalayan salt
- 4 cups broccoli florets
- Cooked basmati rice (for serving)

## DIRECTIONS:

1. Place the tempeh between 2 stacks of paper towels, 4 on top and 4 underneath. Use a large pot or heavy books to press the tempeh from the top for at least 10 minutes. Discard the paper towels, and slice the tempeh into cubes about 1-inch thick.

2. In a small glass bowl, whisk together the corn flour, vegetable stock, sugar, and soy sauce.

3. In a large frying pan over medium-high heat, heat just enough oil to cover the bottom of the pan. When the oil is nice and hot, fry the tempeh in batches for about 4 minutes per side, until it is evenly browned all over. Transfer the fried tempeh to a paper towel-lined plate, and set aside.

4. Discard any excess oil from the pan and return the pan to the heat. Add the spring onions, garlic, and ginger, frying for 2 minutes and allowing the flavors to meld. Stir in the filtered water or additional vegetable stock, with a pinch of salt and the broccoli florets. Reduce the heat to medium, and allow the broccoli to cook with a fitted lid on the pan for 3 minutes, or until the broccoli is done to your liking.

5. Once the broccoli is ready, add the tempeh back to the pan, and stir. Whisk the bowl of corn flour and sauce before adding it to the pan, to ensure all of the corn flour has dissolved. Lumpy corn flour will make for a very unpleasant sauce. Cook the vegetables and sauce for 3-4 minutes while stirring, or until the sauce thickens and coats all of the ingredients.

6. Serve the hot stir-fry over bowls of cooked basmati rice.

# SPICY PAN-SEARED TEMPEH STEAKS

COOK TIME: 20 MINS | MAKES: 4 SERVINGS

## INGREDIENTS:

- 1/2 tsp. cayenne pepper
- 1 1/2 tsp. dried oregano
- 4 tsp. crushed garlic
- 1/4 cup filtered water
- 5 tbsp. red wine vinegar
- 1 lb. tempeh, cut into 3 1/2-inch long by 3/8-inch thick steaks
- 1/2 cup extra-virgin olive oil
- 1 cup fresh parsley leaves, chopped
- Himalayan salt
- Freshly ground black pepper

## DIRECTIONS:

1. In a large, shallow dish, whisk together 1/4 tsp. cayenne pepper, 1 tsp. oregano, 2 tsp. garlic, 1/4 cup water, and 1/4 cup red wine vinegar. Add the tempeh steaks, and toss to coat. Seal the bowl with cling wrap, and chill for a minimum of 60 minutes, or up to 24 hours, gently stirring occasionally to distribute the marinade.

2. In a high-powered food processor, pulse 1/4 cup oil, the parsley, and 1/2 teaspoon salt with the rest of the cayenne pepper, oregano, garlic, and vinegar, until all of the ingredients are roughly chopped and well combined. Scrape the mixture into a bowl, and taste. Add extra salt and pepper as desired.

3. Remove the tempeh from the marinade, and use paper towels to pat off any excess sauce.

4. In a large frying pan over medium heat, heat 2 tablespoons of oil. When the oil is nice and hot, fry 4 tempeh steaks for 2-4 minutes until golden brown. Flip the steaks, and reduce the heat to medium-low, frying the other side for 2-4 minutes until golden. Transfer the steaks to a paper towel-lined plate, and tent to keep warm.

5. Fry the remaining steaks with the remaining oil.

6. Plate the steaks, and serve with the parsley sauce spooned over the top.

# SPICY MUSHROOM TETRAZZINI

COOK TIME: 25-30 MINS | MAKES: 8 SERVINGS

## INGREDIENTS:

- 1/4 cup vegan butter
- 16 oz. button mushrooms, sliced
- 1 shallot, diced
- 6 tsp. crushed garlic
- 2 tbsp. white wine vinegar
- 4 cups vegetable stock
- 1 lb. raw spaghetti
- 1 1/2 cups frozen peas
- 1/4 cup fresh parsley, chopped
- 1 1/2 tsp. Himalayan salt
- 1/2 tsp. freshly ground black pepper
- 1/4 cup panko bread crumbs
- 1/2 cup nutritional yeast
- Crushed red pepper

## DIRECTIONS:

1. In a large pot over medium heat, melt the vegan butter. Add the mushrooms and shallots, frying for 4-6 minutes, or until the mushrooms darken in color. Stir in the garlic, allowing the flavors to meld for 1 minute. Drizzle the vinegar over everything in the pot, and stir for 2-4 minutes until all of the excess liquid has reduced.

2. Pour in the vegetable stock, and bring the pot to a boil while stirring. Once the stock is boiling, add the spaghetti, whole or broken in half. The spaghetti strands should be fully submerged in the stock. Cook the spaghetti, stirring at regular intervals, until the strands have just about reached the desired level of doneness. Stir in the frozen peas, and cook for an additional 2 minutes. The pasta should be cooked to your liking, and the peas thawed and heated all the way through.

3. Without draining the pasta, add the parsley, salt, pepper, bread crumbs, and yeast to the pot, stirring to combine.

4. Spoon the spaghetti and sauce into serving bowls, and garnish with crushed red pepper, if desired, before serving.

# VEGAN-STYLE OVEN STIR-FRY

COOK TIME: 30 MINS | MAKES: 6 SERVINGS

## INGREDIENTS:

- 14 oz. extra-firm tempeh, cubed (½-inch cubes)
- 8 oz. button mushrooms, sliced
- 1/2 head broccoli, cut into bite-sized florets
- 1 red bell pepper, coarsely chopped
- 1/2 red onion, cut into small chunks
- 3 tbsp. tamari
- 2 tbsp. toasted sesame oil
- 1/2 tsp. garlic powder
- 1/2 tsp. Himalayan salt
- 1/4 tsp. ground white pepper
- 1 tsp. Chinese five-spice powder
- Cooked cauliflower rice (for serving)

## DIRECTIONS:

1. Set the oven to preheat to 425°F, with the wire rack in the center of the oven, and line a large, rimmed baking sheet with greaseproof paper.

2. Place the tempeh, mushrooms, broccoli, bell pepper, and red onion in a large mixing bowl, and toss to combine. Add the tamari and toasted sesame oil, and gently toss until everything is evenly coated.

3. In a small glass bowl, whisk together the garlic powder, salt, pepper, and Chinese five-spice powder. Sprinkle the spice mixture over everything in the bowl, and toss to combine.

4. Once everything is evenly coated in the spice mixture, fan the seasoned ingredients out over the prepared baking sheet in an even layer. Bake in the oven for 30 minutes, flipping everything on the sheet half way through the cooking time. The broccoli should be fork-tender and slightly charred around the edges, while the tempeh should be crisp and lightly toasted.

5. Serve the hot stir-fry on a bed of cauliflower rice, and enjoy.

**Quick Tip:**
If you do not have Chinese five-spice powder, omitting it from the recipe will still yield a tasty dish. So don't panic!

# PEPPERS & ZUCCHINI BASIL PASTA

COOK TIME: 15-20 MINS | MAKES: 4 SERVINGS

## INGREDIENTS:

- 1 tsp. cayenne pepper
- 3/4 tsp. Himalayan salt
- 1/4 cup nutritional yeast
- 2 tsp. extra-virgin olive oil
- 1 1/2 tbsp. red wine vinegar
- 4 tsp. crushed garlic
- 12 oz. soft silken tofu
- 1 lb. spaghetti
- 4 medium zucchini
- 1 cup fresh basil leaves, roughly chopped (extra for garnish)
- Red pepper flakes (optional)

## DIRECTIONS:

1. In a high-powered food processor, blend the cayenne pepper, salt, yeast, olive oil, red wine vinegar, garlic, and tofu on high, until you have a lump-free sauce. Scrape the sauce into a small pot, and set aside for later.

2. Prepare the spaghetti according to package instructions. With the spaghetti cooking on the stove, slice the zucchini into strips of roughly the same size as the spaghetti strands. The strands do not have to be exact, but as close as you can get them is preferable.

3. Strain the cooked spaghetti in a colander set over the sink.

4. Heat the sauce in the small pot over low heat until just warmed, but not simmering.

5. Add the strained spaghetti to a large serving bowl, along with the sliced zucchini strands, and scrape the sauce over everything in the bowl. Gently stir until everything is properly combined, and the heat from the sauce has started to wilt the zucchini strands. Add the basil, and stir to combine. Taste, and adjust the seasoning as desired.

6. Plate the pasta, and garnish with extra basil leaves and red pepper flakes for an extra kick, if desired. Serve hot, and enjoy.

# SPICY YAM & SQUASH ENCHILADAS

COOK TIME: 60 MINS | MAKES: 4 SERVINGS

## INGREDIENTS:

**Sauce:**
- 2 tsp. tamari
- 3 tsp. crushed garlic
- 1 1/2 tsp. crushed oregano
- 2 tsp. ground cumin
- 2 tsp. cayenne pepper
- 1/3 cup tomato purée
- 2 1/4 cups vegetable stock
- 1 tbsp. freshly squeezed lime juice

**Filling:**
- 1 lb. yams, chopped into nickel-sized pieces
- 2 tsp. extra-virgin olive oil

- 1/2 small shallot, diced
- 1 cup butternut squash, grated
- 15 oz. canned black turtle beans
- 2 tsp. crushed garlic
- 1/2 tsp. kosher salt
- 1/2 tsp. ground cumin
- 1 tsp. red chili flakes
- 1 tsp. pure maple syrup
- 8 corn or flour tortillas, warmed
- Fresh coriander leaves, chopped
- Avocado, sliced (for garnish)

## DIRECTIONS:

1. In a small pot over medium-low heat, whisk together the tamari, garlic, oregano, cumin, cayenne pepper, tomato purée, and vegetable stock, until the sauce begins to simmer. Adjust the heat to maintain a gentle simmer for 10-15 minutes, or until the sauce begins to thicken. Turn off the heat, and whisk in the lime juice. Allow to cool slightly while you prepare the rest of the dish.

2. Place a colander over a pot of rapidly boiling water. The bottom of the colander should not be touching the water. Place the yams in the colander, and cover with a fitted lid. Steam the yams for 10-15 minutes, or until they are fork-tender. Place the steamed yams in a large bowl, and mash. You may leave a few chunks for texture if desired.

3. Meanwhile, in a large frying pan over medium heat, heat the olive oil. When the oil is nice and hot, fry the shallots for 3-5 minutes until the edges begin to caramelize. Add the squash, and stir for 1 minute. Add the black beans, crushed garlic, salt, cumin, and red chili flakes, stirring for an additional 2 minutes. Turn off the heat, and gently stir in the mashed yams and pure maple syrup, until properly combined.

4. Set the oven to preheat to 375°F, with the wire rack in the center of the oven.

5. Add 1 ½ cups of the slightly cooled sauce to the bottom of a large casserole dish in an even layer. Lightly spread a small amount of sauce onto each wrap, before spooning the filling onto the wraps in equal amounts. Tightly fold the wraps like burritos, and place them in the dish, seam side down. The enchiladas should be tightly packed together. Spoon the rest of the sauce over all of the enchiladas.

6. Cover the dish with tinfoil, and bake in the oven for 20 minutes. After 2o minutes, remove the foil and bake the enchiladas for an additional 5 minutes.

7. Serve the cooked enchiladas hot, garnished with fresh coriander leaves and sliced avocado.

# TRIPLE-THREAT INDONESIAN FRIED RICE

COOK TIME: 25 MINS | MAKES: 2 SERVINGS

## INGREDIENTS:

- 3 cups cooked rice, cooled
- 7 oz. extra-firm tempeh
- 2 tbsp. extra-virgin olive oil
- 1 small shallot, diced
- 4 tsp. crushed garlic
- 2 tsp. red chili flakes
- 1 small red bell pepper, diced
- 1/3 cup diced carrots
- 1/4 cup frozen peas
- 3 tbsp. sweet vegan soy sauce
- Kosher salt
- Freshly ground black pepper
- Spring onions, chopped (for garnish)
- Cucumber, sliced (for garnish)
- Heirloom tomatoes, sliced (for garnish)

## DIRECTIONS:

1. Place the cooked and cooled rice in a large mixing bowl, and use a fork to fluff it and separate the grains.

2. Place the tempeh between two layers of paper towels, and press with a heavy object for at least 10 minutes. Slice the tempeh into 1/2-inch cubes.

3. In a large frying pan over medium-high heat, heat the olive oil. When the oil is nice and hot, fry the tempeh cubes for 10 minutes until golden brown on all sides, flipping every 2 minutes to prevent burning.

4. Stir in the shallots, and fry for 3 minutes. Add the garlic and chili flakes, allowing the flavors to meld for 2 minutes.

5. Toss in the peppers, carrots, and peas, frying for 5 minutes, or until the vegetables are fork-tender.

6. Add the sweet soy sauce and bowl of fluffed rice to the pan, stirring to combine. Taste the rice, and season with salt and pepper as desired. Cook the rice for 2-3 minutes until heated through.

7. Serve hot, garnished with spring onions, cucumber, and tomatoes.

# MADEIRA-GLAZED SHEPHERD'S PIE

COOK TIME: 30-40 MINS | MAKES: 4-6 SERVINGS

## INGREDIENTS:

- 2 lbs. Yukon gold potatoes, peeled and cubed (1-inch cubes)
- Kosher salt
- 1/4 cup fresh chives, minced
- 5 tbsp. extra-virgin olive oil
- 1/3 cup unsweetened almond milk
- 1 tsp. baking powder
- 4 oz. button mushrooms, chopped
- 1 shallot, chopped
- Ground white pepper
- 2 tsp. crushed garlic

- 1 tbsp. tomato paste
- 2 tbsp. Madeira
- 2 tbsp. all-purpose flour
- 1 whole bay leaf
- 2 fresh thyme sprigs
- 2 tsp. vegan Worcestershire sauce
- 2 carrots, peeled and chopped
- 2 1/2 cups vegetable stock
- 12 oz. vegan protein crumbles, broken into small pieces

## DIRECTIONS:

1. Place the potato cubes in a large pot, add 1 tablespoon salt, and cover with water. Bring the water to a gentle simmer over medium-high heat. Once the water begins to simmer, adjust the heat to maintain a gentle simmer for 8-10 minutes, or until the potatoes are fork-tender all the way through.

2. Strain all the water from the potatoes. In the same pot, mash the potatoes with the chives, 1/4 cup olive oil, almond milk, and baking powder until the potatoes are light and fluffy. Baking powder is an old secret to fluffy mashed potatoes.

3. In a large, oven-safe frying pan, heat the remaining oil. When the oil is nice and hot, fry the mushrooms and shallots with 1/4 teaspoon pepper for 5 minutes, or until the mushrooms darken in color and the shallot becomes translucent. Add the crushed garlic and tomato paste, stirring for 2 minutes until the bottom of the pan begins to glaze.

4. Add the Madeira, and deglaze the pan for 1 minute, scraping up any bits of food that may have stuck to the bottom of the pan. The liquid should evaporate by at least half during this time. Stir the flour through the sauce for 1 additional minute. Add the bay leaf, thyme, Worcestershire sauce, carrots, and vegetable stock, stirring and deglazing the pan until the sauce begins to boil. Lower the heat to medium-low, and maintain a gentle simmer for 10-15 minutes. Remove and discard the thyme sprigs and bay leaf. Taste, and season with additional salt and pepper as desired.

5. Preheat the oven broiler with the wire rack 5 inches away from the element.

6. Carefully spoon the mashed potatoes over the sauce in the pan in an even layer, making sure that the mash touches the sides of the pan, sealing the sauce at the bottom. Use a fork to draw patterns in the mash. Alternatively, use a piping bag to pipe the mash onto the sauce in whatever pattern you desire. Broil the pie in the oven for 5-10 minutes, or until the mash is lightly browned on the tips.

7. Serve hot.

# VEGAN-STYLE PEPPERONCINI PIZZA

COOK TIME: 15-20 MINS | MAKES: 4 SERVINGS

## INGREDIENTS:

**Sauce:**
- 1/4 tsp. Himalayan salt
- 2 tbsp. extra-virgin olive oil
- 2 tsp. crushed garlic
- 1 tsp. dried oregano
- 28 oz. canned whole, peeled tomatoes

**Pizza:**
- All-purpose flour (for dusting)
- 1 lb. pizza dough, at room temperature

- 1/4 cup pepperoncini peppers, sliced
- 1 small shallot, thinly sliced
- 8 oz. button mushrooms, thinly sliced
- 1 cup grape tomatoes, halved
- 1/4 tsp. flaky sea salt
- 1/8 tsp. ground white pepper
- 1/2 tsp. dried oregano
- 2 tbsp. extra-virgin olive oil (more for greasing)
- Fresh basil leaves (for serving)

## DIRECTIONS:

1. Set the oven to preheat to 500°F, with the wire rack in the center of the oven.

2. On a lightly-floured surface, divide the dough in half, and press the halves into 2 smooth balls. Cover the dough balls with a slightly damp cloth, and allow the dough to rest while you prepare the rest of the dish.

3. Place the salt, olive oil, garlic, oregano, and whole tomatoes in a high-powered food processor, reserving the juice from the can for another recipe, or simply discarding it. Blend on high until you have a smooth sauce.

4. In a large mixing bowl, toss together the peppers, shallot, mushrooms, grape tomatoes, salt, pepper, oregano, and oil until all of the ingredients are evenly coated.

5. Lightly grease a large, rimmed baking sheet and set aside.

6. On a lightly floured surface, roll the dough into two pizzas, each 10-inches wide. Arrange the pizza bases on the prepared baking sheet.

7. Place 3 tablespoons of the sauce on each base, and spread it out evenly. Be sure to leave a border of about 1\2 inch around the edge of each pizza base.

8. Divide the vegetables between the two pizza bases, arranging them in an even layer on each one.

9. Bake the pizzas in the oven for 15-20 minutes, or until the base is a crispy golden brown.

10. Garnish the pizzas with fresh basil leaves, slice, and serve.

**Quick Tip:**
This sauce recipe makes more than enough sauce for a few uses, so be sure to freeze the extra sauce in an airtight container for future use.

# DECADENT & LUSH MUSHROOM BOLOGNESE

COOK TIME: 30-40 MINS | MAKES: 4-6 SERVINGS

## INGREDIENTS:

- 1 carrot, peeled and chopped
- 1 small shallot
- 2 lbs. Cremini mushrooms, peeled and quartered
- 28 oz. canned whole, peeled tomatoes
- 3 tbsp. extra-virgin avocado oil
- 1/2 oz. dried porcini mushrooms, rinsed and minced
- 1 tbsp. kikkoman soy sauce
- 1/2 cup vegetable stock
- 1 cup dry red wine
- 2 tbsp. tomato paste
- 1 tsp. mixed Italian herbs
- 1 tsp. organic dark brown sugar
- 3 tsp. crushed garlic
- Kosher salt
- Ground white pepper
- 3 tbsp. unsweetened soy creamer
- 1 lb. uncooked spaghetti

## DIRECTIONS:

1. In a high-powered food processor, pulse the carrots on high until the pieces are no larger than 1/2 inch. Work in batches if the carrots do not all fit in the processor. Scrape the chopped carrots into a large mixing bowl, and repeat the process with the shallot and Cremini mushrooms. Scrape the vegetables into the bowl of carrots once chopped.

2. Place the canned tomatoes, with their sauce, in a clean food processor, and blend on high until the tomatoes are finely chopped. Scrape the chopped tomatoes into their own bowl, and set aside.

3. In a large pot over medium heat, heat the avocado oil. When the oil is nice and hot, add the chopped vegetables from the bowl, along with the porcini mushrooms, and fry for 5 minutes, until all of the mushrooms darken in color. Increase the heat to medium-high, and fry the vegetables and mushrooms for 12-15 minutes until the vegetables are just beginning to brown around the edges. Stir at regular intervals to prevent burning.

4. Add the chopped tomatoes, soy sauce, vegetable stock, dry red wine, tomato paste, Italian herbs, brown sugar, garlic, 1/2 teaspoon salt, and 1/4 teaspoon pepper, and stir to combine. Once the sauce begins to simmer, reduce the heat to maintain a gentle simmer for 8-10 minutes until the sauce thickens. Be careful not to cook the sauce too long or let too much liquid evaporate. Turn off the heat and add the soy creamer, stirring to combine.

5. Bring 4 quarts of water to a rolling boil in a large pot, and add 1 tablespoon of salt. Add the spaghetti, and cook according to package instructions, or until the strands reach the desired level of doneness. When the spaghetti is cooked, reserve 1/2 cup of the spaghetti water before straining through a colander set over the sink.

6. Return the spaghetti to the pot, and toss with the mushroom sauce. If the sauce is too thick, add a little of the reserved spaghetti water at a time and stir, until the sauce is to your liking. Taste, and adjust the seasoning as desired.

7. Plate the spaghetti, and serve hot.

# SPICY CHICKPEA TIKKA MASALA

COOK TIME: 40 MINS | MAKES: 6-8 SERVINGS

## INGREDIENTS:

- 1\4 tsp. cayenne pepper
- 1 tsp. sweet smoked paprika
- 1/2 tsp. ground turmeric
- 1 tsp. ground cumin
- 1 tsp. ground masala
- 1 tsp. ground cilantro seeds
- 1 tsp. kosher salt
- 3 tbsp. extra-virgin olive oil
- 1 shallot, finely chopped
- 3 tsp. crushed garlic
- 1 tsp. freshly grated ginger
- 28 oz. canned tomato paste

- 2 tsp. organic dark brown sugar
- 1 1/2 cups vegetable stock
- 1 cup green beans, trimmed
- 1 cup okra, diced
- 2 cups cauliflower florets
- 2 cups canned chickpeas, rinsed and drained
- 3 carrots, diced
- 1/2 cup peas
- 1 cup cashew heavy cream
- 1/2 cup fresh coriander leaves, chopped (more for garnish)
- Jasmine rice, cooked (for serving)

## DIRECTIONS:

1. In a small glass bowl, stir together the cayenne pepper, sweet smoked paprika, turmeric, cumin, masala, cilantro seeds, and salt. Set the bowl aside on the counter while you prepare the rest of the dish.

2. In a large pot over medium-high heat, heat the olive oil. When the oil is nice and hot, fry the shallots for 2 minutes until the edges are just becoming translucent. Stir in the garlic and ginger for 30 seconds, allowing the flavors to meld. Add the spice mixture after reducing the heat to medium, and stir for 1-2 minutes until the mixture becomes very fragrant. This step helps bring out the flavors of any spice that has been standing on the shelf for too long. Stir in the tomato paste for 1 minute, then add the sugar and vegetable stock, and stir until all of the ingredients are properly combined in a fragrant sauce.

3. Bring the heat back up to medium-high, and stir in the green beans, okra, cauliflower, chickpeas, and carrots. When the sauce begins to simmer, lower the heat to maintain a gentle simmer, with the lid on the pot, for 20-30 minutes until the vegetables are properly cooked. Stir at regular intervals to prevent burning. Add the peas and stir again.

4. Gradually whisk in the cashew heavy cream. Allow the sauce to gently simmer for 5 minutes before adding the fresh coriander leaves and stirring to combine. Taste the sauce, and adjust the seasoning as desired.

5. Serve the tikka masala over a bed of hot jasmine rice, garnished with extra coriander leaves.

# CURRIES, SOUPS, & STEWS

# SPICY PUMPKIN & CHARD SOUP

COOK TIME: 60 MINS | MAKES: 4-6 SERVINGS

## INGREDIENTS:

- 2 carrots, diced
- 2 celery stalks, diced
- 1 shallot, diced
- 1 cup pumpkin, peeled and diced
- 1/4 cup filtered water (if needed)
- 1/2 tsp. ground white pepper
- 1 tsp. ground turmeric
- 1 tsp. cayenne pepper
- 2 tsp. kosher salt
- 5 tsp. crushed garlic
- 1 tsp. freshly grated ginger
- 8 cups vegetable stock
- 1 cup uncooked brown rice
- 3 lemons
- 6 cups Swiss chard, chopped

## DIRECTIONS:

1. Heat a large soup pot over medium-high heat. When the pot is nice and hot, add the carrots, celery, shallots, and pumpkin, and dry cook for 8-10 minutes while stirring, until the vegetables just begin to crisp around the edges. Add the water only if the vegetables are sticking to the bottom of the pot, and cook until all the water is gone.

2. Stir in the white pepper, turmeric, cayenne pepper, salt, garlic, and ginger for 30 seconds, allowing the flavors to meld. Add the vegetable stock, and stir to combine until the soup begins to simmer.

3. Add the rice and half a lemon, stirring to combine. Place a fitted lid on the pot, and cook for 30 minutes, stirring at regular intervals, or until the rice is cooked to your liking. Working in batches, add the Swiss chard to the soup, and stir. Wait till each batch of chard has wilted before adding more. When all of the chard is in the pot, cover and simmer for an additional 5-10 minutes until the chard is properly cooked.

4. Discard the lemon half, and stir in the juice from the remaining 2 1/2 lemons.

5. Ladle the soup into bowls, and serve hot.

**Quick Tip:**
Any leftover soup can be stored in the fridge in an airtight container for no more than 5 days.

# QUICK & EASY LENTIL & VEG SOUP

COOK TIME: 15-20 MINS | MAKES: 6-8 SERVINGS

## INGREDIENTS:

- 1 tbsp. extra-virgin olive oil
- 2 carrots, peeled and thinly sliced
- 2 celery stalks, thinly sliced
- 1 shallot, diced
- 4 tsp. crushed garlic
- 1 Yukon gold potato, peeled and cubed (1/2 inch cubes)
- 6 cups vegetable stock
- 1 tsp. dried oregano
- 1 tsp. kosher salt
- 1/2 tsp. freshly ground black pepper
- 1 1/2 cups Swiss chard, roughly chopped
- 14.5 oz. diced tomatoes
- 15 oz. canned lentils, drained and rinsed
- 3 cups broccoli florets
- 1 cup frozen corn

## DIRECTIONS:

1. Heat the olive oil in a large soup pot over medium heat. When the oil is nice and hot, fry the carrots, celery, and shallots for 3 minutes, or until the shallots become translucent. Add the garlic, and stir for 1 minute, allowing the flavors to meld.

2. Stir in the potato cubes and vegetable stock. Place a lid on the pot, and bring the soup to a boil. Once the soup begins to boil, lower the heat to maintain a gentle simmer for 6-8 minutes, or until the potatoes are cooked all the way through.

3. Add the oregano, salt, pepper, chard, diced tomatoes, lentils, broccoli, and corn. Bring the soup back up to a simmer while stirring. Simmer the soup for 2-4 minutes until the vegetables have softened.

4. Ladle the soup into bowls, and serve hot.

**Quick Tip:**
If you do not like canned lentils, cook dried lentils according to the package instructions, and add 1 1/2 cups.

# VEGAN-STYLE THAI GREEN CURRY

COOK TIME: 20 MINS | MAKES: 3 SERVINGS

## INGREDIENTS:

- 7 oz. extra-firm tempeh
- 1 tbsp. extra-virgin olive oil
- 2 tsp. freshly grated ginger
- 2 tsp. crushed garlic
- 3-4 tbsp. green curry paste
- 1/2 cup vegetable stock (more if needed)
- 13.5 oz. canned full fat coconut milk
- 1 1/2 tbsp. dark brown sugar
- 1 tsp. Kikkoman soy sauce
- 1 small red bell pepper, seeded and sliced into strips
- 7 oz. canned baby corn, halved lengthwise
- 1 medium Chinese eggplant, sliced into 1 1/2-inch rounds
- 15 fresh Thai basil leaves
- Basmati rice, steamed (for serving)
- Freshly squeezed lime juice
- Fresh coriander leaves, chopped (for garnish)

## DIRECTIONS:

1. Place the tempeh between 2 stacks of paper towels, 4 on top and 4 underneath. Use a heavy pot or stack of books to press the tempeh for at least 10 minutes. Discard the paper towels, and slice the tempeh into 1-inch cubes.

2. Heat the oil in a large pot over medium-high heat. When the oil is nice and hot, fry the ginger and garlic for 2 minutes, allowing the flavors to meld. Add the curry paste according to taste, and cook for an additional 3-4 minutes until the mixture is very fragrant. Gradually whisk in the stock and coconut milk, until the paste has disappeared into the soup. Add the sugar and soy sauce, then stir and taste, adjusting the seasoning as desired. Bring the soup to a simmer, and adjust the heat to maintain a gentle simmer for 4 minutes.

3. Stir in the tempeh cubes, bell pepper, corn, and Chinese eggplant. Allow the soup to cook for 5 minutes with the lid on the pot, or until the vegetables are properly cooked.

4. Taste the soup and adjust the seasoning. If the soup is not thin enough for your liking, add additional vegetable stock, and stir until heated through.

5. Transfer the pot to a wooden chopping board, and stir in the basil leaves.

6. Ladle the soup into bowls of steamed basmati rice, and serve sprinkled with lime juice and fresh coriander leaves.

# CHEESY FRENCH ONION BROTH

COOK TIME: 40 MINS | MAKES: 4 SERVINGS

## INGREDIENTS:

- 2 tbsp. extra-virgin olive oil
- 8 cups yellow onions, thinly sliced
- 2 tsp. kosher salt
- 1 tsp. freshly ground black pepper
- 1/4 tsp. ground white pepper
- 1 cup dry red wine
- 1 fresh rosemary sprig
- 2 fresh thyme sprigs
- 1 whole bay leaf
- 2 mushroom bouillon cubes
- 4 cups filtered water
- 1/4 cup dry sherry
- 8 oz. vegan cream cheese
- 8 1/2-inch thick slices vegan bread, lightly toasted
- Fresh parsley, chopped (for garnish)

## DIRECTIONS:

1. Heat the oil in a large soup pot over medium-low heat. When the oil is nice and hot, fry the onions for 20-30 minutes until nicely caramelized. Don't attempt to fry the onions too quickly, as slow roasting them adds to the soup's flavor. Season the onions with salt, black pepper, and white pepper.

2. Bring the heat up to medium-high, and stir in the wine. Stir the pot for 2 minutes, or until some of the wine has evaporated. Stir in the rosemary, thyme, bay leaf, bouillon cubes, and filtered water. When the broth begins to simmer, add the sherry, and stir for 2 minutes while simmering. Remove and discard the fresh herb sprigs and bay leaf.

3. Preheat the oven broiler to high with the wire rack one slot down from the top. Arrange 4 oven-safe bowls on a large, rimmed baking sheet.

4. Spoon the broth into the 4 bowls set on the baking sheet, filling to about an inch below the rim. Spread a generous amount of cream cheese over each slice of bread, and lay 2 slices of bread, side by side, on top of each bowl of soup. Transfer the sheet to the oven, and broil the broth and bread for 2-3 minutes, or until the cream cheese is bubbling.

5. Allow the broth and toast to cool on the counter for 5 minutes, and serve garnished with fresh parsley.

# VEGAN CHILI WITH A TWIST

COOK TIME: 50-60 MINS | MAKES: 6 SERVINGS

## INGREDIENTS:

- 1 tsp. ground white pepper
- 1 tsp. dried oregano
- 1 tsp. ground cumin
- 1 tsp. cayenne pepper
- 1 tsp. unsweetened cocoa powder
- 2 tsp. kosher salt
- 2 tsp. chili powder
- 2 tsp. sweet smoked paprika
- 1 tbsp. organic dark brown sugar
- 2 tbsp. extra-virgin olive oil
- 2 celery stalks, diced
- 1 green bell pepper, seeded and diced
- 1 shallot, diced
- 3 tsp. crushed garlic

- 6 oz. canned tomato paste
- 4 cups vegetable stock
- 1 whole bay leaf
- 2 tsp. liquid aminos
- 1 tbsp. balsamic vinegar
- 3 cups canned black turtle beans, drained
- 3 cups green lentils, rinsed and drained

**Toppings:**
- Sliced spring onions
- Sliced avocado
- Chopped fresh parsley
- Chopped fresh coriander leaves
- Vegan sour cream
- Sliced fresh tomatoes

## DIRECTIONS:

1. In a small glass bowl, whisk together the pepper, oregano, cumin, cayenne pepper, cocoa powder, salt, chili powder, sweet smoked paprika, and dark brown sugar. Set aside.

2. Heat the oil in a large pot over medium-high heat. When the oil is nice and hot, fry the celery, bell pepper, and shallots for 5-7 minutes, or until the shallots lose their color. Stir in the garlic for 30 seconds, allowing the flavors to meld.

3. Add the spice blend and tomato paste, stirring for 1-2 minutes until the paste begins to brown. Add the stock, and stir. Deglaze the pot by scraping up any bits of food that may have gotten stuck to the bottom. Add the bay leaf, liquid aminos, vinegar, beans, and lentils. Stir, and bring the broth up to a gentle simmer. Adjust the heat to maintain a gentle simmer for 30-40 minutes with the lid on the pot, or until the broth has thickened. Discard the bay leaf.

4. Spoon the chili into bowls, and serve hot with toppings of your choice.

**Quick Tip:**
Any leftovers can be refrigerated in an airtight container for no more than 7 days.

# CREAMY CASHEW & CHICKPEA SOUP

COOK TIME: 25 MINS | MAKES: 6-8 SERVINGS

## INGREDIENTS:

- 2 tbsp. extra-virgin avocado oil
- 2 celery stalks, thinly sliced
- 2 carrots, thinly sliced
- 1 shallot, chopped
- 4 tsp. crushed garlic
- 5 cups vegetable stock
- 2 Yukon gold potatoes, skinned and cubed (bite-sized cubes)
- 1 1/2 tsp. kosher salt (more if needed)
- 1 1/2 tsp. poultry seasoning
- 1 cup raw cashews, soaked or boiled until soft
- 1 tbsp. balsamic vinegar
- 1 tsp. ground white pepper (more if needed)
- 15 oz. canned chickpeas, rinsed and drained
- 1 cup frozen corn
- 1 cup frozen peas
- Spring onions, coarsely chopped

## DIRECTIONS:

1. Heat the oil in a large pot over medium heat. When the oil is nice and hot, fry the celery, carrots, and shallots for 3-5 minutes, or until the shallots soften. Stir in the garlic, allowing the flavors to meld for 1 minute.

2. Stir in the potatoes and 4 cups of vegetable stock. Once the stock begins to simmer, lower the heat to maintain a gentle simmer with the lid on the pot for 8-10 minutes, or until the potatoes are cooked all the way through. Be careful not to overcook the potatoes, or they will disappear later in the cooking process.

3. Meanwhile, in a high-powered food processor, blend the remaining stock, the salt, poultry seasoning, and cashews on high, until you have a lump-free paste. Scrape the paste into the pot, and stir to combine.

4. Stir in the vinegar, pepper, chickpeas, corn, and peas. Once the soup begins to simmer, stir for 4 minutes until all of the ingredients are heated through. Taste the soup, and season with additional salt and pepper if desired.

5. Ladle the soup into bowls, and serve hot, garnished with spring onions.

# SOUPY MUSHROOM & CORN CHOWDER

COOK TIME: 30 MINS | MAKES: 6 SERVINGS

## INGREDIENTS:

- 2 tbsp. extra-virgin avocado oil
- 8 oz. button mushrooms, sliced
- 2 celery stalks, chopped
- 2 carrots, peeled and thinly sliced
- 4 tsp. crushed garlic
- 1 shallot, chopped
- 2 tbsp. tomato paste
- 4 cups vegetable stock
- 2 Yukon gold potatoes, peeled and cubed (1/2-inch cubes)
- 1 cup filtered water
- 3/4 cup raw cashews, soaked or boiled until soft
- 1/2 lemon, juiced
- 1/2 tsp. ground white pepper
- 1 1/2 tsp. Himalayan salt
- 2 tsp. Old Bay seasoning
- 1 1/2 cups corn
- Fresh chives, chopped (for garnish)
- Oyster crackers (for serving)

## DIRECTIONS:

1. In a large pot over medium heat, heat the oil. When the oil is nice and hot, fry the mushrooms, celery, carrots, garlic, and shallots for 4-6 minutes, or until the mushrooms darken in color and the shallots become translucent.

2. Stir in the tomato paste for 1 minute until all the vegetables are evenly coated. Add the stock and potatoes. Bring the stock up to a simmer, and lower the heat to maintain a gentle simmer for 6-8 minutes with the lid on the pot, or until the potatoes are cooked all the way through, but not completely soft.

3. In a high-powered food processor, blend the filtered water and cashews on high until you have a lump-free paste. Scrape the paste into the soup, and add the lemon juice, pepper, salt, Old Bay seasoning, and corn, stirring to combine.

4. Bring the soup back up to a simmer for 4-6 minutes, or until it has thickened into a chowder-like consistency. Taste the soup, and adjust the seasoning as desired.

5. Ladle into bowls, and serve garnished with fresh chives. Serve oyster crackers on the side if desired.

# LIME & MANGO THAI CURRY

COOK TIME: 10-15 MINUTES | MAKES: 4 SERVINGS

## INGREDIENTS:

- 1 tsp. extra-virgin olive oil
- 1/2 shallot, chopped
- 1 red bell pepper, chopped
- 1 medium zucchini, sliced into 1/8-inch crescents
- 1 1/2 cups green beans, sliced onto 1/2-inch pieces
- 2 tbsp. red curry paste
- 1 1/2 tbsp. fresh ginger, minced
- 3 tsp. crushed garlic
- 1 cup vegetable stock
- 1 1/2 cups canned full-cream coconut milk
- 1 tbsp. tamari
- 3 oz. Dry-fried tofu
- 1 ripe mango, cut into chunks
- 2 tbsp. freshly squeezed lime juice
- Basmati rice, cooked (for serving)

## DIRECTIONS:

1. Heat the oil in a medium pot over medium heat. When the oil is nice and hot, fry the shallots for 3 minutes until the edges just begin to lose their color. Stir in the bell pepper, zucchini, and green beans for 2-3 minutes, or until the vegetables start to soften. Add the curry paste, ginger, and garlic, stirring for 30 seconds and allowing the flavors to meld.

2. Stir in the stock, coconut milk, and tamari, and bring the sauce up to a gentle simmer.

3. Add the tofu and mango chunks. Lower the heat to maintain a gentle simmer for 5-8 minutes. Turn off the heat and stir in the freshly squeezed lime juice.

4. Ladle the curry into bowls of cooked basmati rice, and serve.

# OLD-SCHOOL SOUTHWESTERN SOUP

COOK TIME: 15-20 MINS | MAKES: 4-6 SERVINGS

## INGREDIENTS:

- 1 tbsp. extra-virgin olive oil
- 1 shallot, diced
- 1 red bell pepper, diced
- 1 carrot, diced
- 1/8 tsp. kosher salt
- 1 tsp. cayenne pepper
- 2 1/2 tsp. dried oregano
- 2 1/2 tsp. ground cumin
- 4 tsp. crushed garlic
- 1-2 jalapeños, minced
- 1/4 cup tomato paste
- 14.5 oz. canned low-salt diced tomatoes
- 5 cups vegetable stock
- 6-8 corn wraps, sliced into 1-inch squares
- 1 tbsp. freshly squeezed lime juice
- 1 1/2 cups cooked chickpeas
- Fresh coriander leaves, chopped (for garnish) (optional)
- Avocado, sliced (for garnish) (optional)
- Jalapeños, chopped (for garnish) (optional)

## DIRECTIONS:

1. In a large pot over medium heat, heat the olive oil. When the oil is nice and hot, fry the shallots for 2 minutes, or until they become translucent. Stir in the bell pepper and carrot for 3 minutes until the vegetables start to brown.

2. Stir in the salt, cayenne pepper, oregano, cumin, garlic, and minced jalapeños, allowing the flavors to meld for 30 seconds. Add the tomato paste and diced tomatoes, stirring until all the ingredients are properly combined. Stir in the stock, and bring the soup to a gentle simmer.

3. Add the lime juice and wrap pieces, allowing the soup to simmer for 10 minutes until the squares soften. Use a handheld immersion blender to blend all of the ingredients into a lump-free soup. If you do not own an immersion blender, simply blend the soup in a normal blender, and return it to the pot.

4. Ladle the soup into bowls, and add a generous helping of cooked chickpeas.

5. Serve the soup hot, garnished with toppings of your choice.

# SIMPLE BUTTERNUT SOUP

COOK TIME: 25 MINS | MAKES: 4 SERVINGS

## INGREDIENTS:

- 1 1/2 tbsp. extra-virgin olive oil
- 1 carrot, sliced into thin half-moons
- 2 celery stalks, chopped
- 1/2 shallot, chopped
- 3 tsp. crushed garlic
- 3 large butternut squash, sliced into 1/8-inch thick slices
- 1 medium Yukon gold potato, sliced into small cubes
- 4 cups vegetable stock
- 1/2 tsp. kosher salt
- 1/3 cup spring onions, sliced

## DIRECTIONS:

1. Heat the oil in a large pot over medium heat. When the oil is nice and hot, fry the carrots, celery, and shallots for 3-5 minutes, or until the shallots are nicely caramelized. Stir in the garlic, butternut, and potatoes, and cook for an additional 3 minutes.

2. Add the stock and salt, stirring until the soup begins to boil. Lower the heat to maintain a gentle simmer for 10-15 minutes, until the potatoes are cooked all the way through and the carrots are fork-tender.

3. Use a handheld immersion blender to puree the soup. You may leave a few chunks for texture if you like. If you do not own an immersion blender, simply transfer the soup to a normal blender and blend well before returning the soup to the pot.

4. Stir in the chives, and taste. Adjust the seasoning as desired.

5. Ladle the soup into bowls, and serve hot.

**Quick Tip:**
Leave the skin on the butternut for added vitamins.

# VEGAN-STYLE KIMCHI STEW

COOK TIME: 20 MINS | MAKES: 4 SERVINGS

## INGREDIENTS:

- 7 oz. extra-firm tempeh
- 1 tbsp. hon mirin
- Ground white pepper
- 1/2 tsp. crushed garlic
- 2 tsp. red chili paste
- 2 tbsp. tamari
- 2 tbsp. chili powder
- 1 tbsp. toasted sesame oil
- 3 spring onions, thinly sliced (extra for garnish)
- 1 medium shallot, sliced
- 1 cup aged vegan kimchi
- 4 medium shiitake mushrooms, sliced
- 3 cups vegetable broth
- Steamed basmati rice for serving

## DIRECTIONS:

1. Place the tempeh between two stacks of paper towels, 4 above and 4 below. Using a large pot or heavy stack of books, press the tempeh for a minimum of 10 minutes. Discard the paper towels, and slice the tempeh into 1 inch thick slices.

2. In a small glass bowl, whisk together the hon mirin, white pepper, crushed garlic, red chili paste, tamari, and chili powder until you have a smooth paste. Set the bowl aside while you prepared the rest of the dish.

3. Heat the sesame oil in a large pot over medium heat. When the oil is nice and hot, fry the spring onions and shallots for 2-3 minutes, or until the shallots become translucent. Stir in the soup paste and vegan kimchi for 2 minutes. Add the pressed tempeh and shiitake mushrooms. Pour the broth over everything in the pot, and raise the heat to medium-high. Simmer the broth for 5-6 minutes, adjusting the heat as needed.

4. Taste the soup, and adjust the seasoning if desired.

5. Serve the stew in bowls of steamed basmati rice, garnished with extra spring onions if desired.

# BRAISED IMPOSTER PORK

COOK TIME: 30 MINS | MAKES: 3 SERVINGS

## INGREDIENTS:

- 14 oz. extra-firm tempeh
- 2 tbsp. extra-virgin olive oil
- 2 tbsp. organic dark brown sugar
- 3 tsp. crushed garlic
- 1 small white onion, finely chopped
- 1 tsp. dark soy sauce
- 1/4 tsp. freshly ground black pepper
- 1 tsp. Chinese five-spice powder
- 2 tbsp. dry sherry
- 1/8 - 1/4 tsp. Szechuan pepper powder

- 3 tbsp. kikkoman soy sauce
- 8 oz. shiitake mushrooms, finely diced
- 1 1/2 cups vegetable stock
- 2 tbsp. filtered water, room temperature
- 1 tbsp. corn flour
- Steamed jasmine rice (for serving)
- Spring onions, chopped (for garnish)
- Blanched Bok choy leaves

## DIRECTIONS:

1. Place the tempeh between 2 stacks of paper towels, 4 at the bottom and 4 on top. Use a heavy pot or stack of books to press the tempeh for at least 10 minutes. Discard the paper towels, and crumble the tempeh into a large mixing bowl until the pieces resemble ground pork.

2. Heat the oil in a large frying pan over medium-high heat. When the oil is nice and hot, lower the heat to medium and add the dark brown sugar, stirring for 3 minutes until the sugar has dissolved into a brown liquid.

3. Stir in the garlic and onions, frying for 2 minutes until the onions are cooked all the way through.

4. Raise the heat to high, and stir in the crumbled tempeh, dark soy sauce, black pepper, five-spice, dry sherry, Szechuan pepper, and soy sauce until all of the ingredients are properly combined. Stir until the sherry cooks away. Lower the heat, add the shiitake mushrooms, and cook for an additional 2 minutes. Lower the heat back down to medium-high, and cook for an additional 6-8 minutes, or until the extra water from the tempeh has cooked away, and the pieces resemble browned pork. Add the stock, and stir for an additional 2 minutes until the stock reduces.

5. In a small glass bowl, whisk together the filtered water and corn flour until you have a smooth paste. Gradually whisk the corn flour paste into the pan for 1 minute, until the sauce begins to thicken. Reduce the heat to medium, and simmer the tempeh for 2 minutes. Taste the tempeh, and adjust the seasoning as desired.

6. Serve the tempeh pork over a bowl of hot jasmine rice, garnished with spring onions and Bok choy leaves.

# COMFY & COZY CAULIFLOWER CURRY

COOK TIME: 45 MINS | MAKES: 4 SERVINGS

## INGREDIENTS:

- 4 tbsp. extra-virgin avocado oil
- 2 medium shallots, thinly sliced
- 1 1/4 tsp. Himalayan salt (divided)
- 1 jalapeño, halved and seeded
- 2 tsp. crushed garlic
- 1 tsp. freshly grated ginger
- 1 tbsp. curry powder
- 2 tbsp. tomato paste
- 3/4 cup filtered water
- 13.5 oz. canned full-fat coconut milk
- 1 large cauliflower head, chopped into small florets
- Steamed jasmine rice (for serving)
- Fresh coriander leaves, chopped (for garnish)
- Lightly toasted cashews, roughly chopped (for garnish)
- 1 cup sugar snap peas, thinly sliced (for garnish)
- Lime wedges (for serving)

## DIRECTIONS:

1. Heat 3 tablespoons of oil in a large pot over medium-high heat. When the oil is nice and hot, add the shallots and 1/2 teaspoon salt, stirring until the shallots are evenly coated in the oil. Place a lid on the pot, and steam for 5-6 minutes. Remove the lid and fry the shallots, stirring at regular intervals, for 12 minutes until the onions are nicely caramelized.

2. Meanwhile, place the remaining oil, the jalapeño, garlic, and ginger in a blender, and blend on high until you have a smooth paste.

3. Scrape the paste into the pot, and fry for 1-2 minutes, allowing the flavors to meld while you scrape the bottom of the pot. Stir in the curry powder and tomato paste for 30 seconds.

4. Add the remaining salt, the filtered water, and the coconut milk. Add the cauliflower florets, and stir until the sauce is boiling. Lower the heat to maintain a gentle simmer for 12-15 minutes with the lid on the pot, or until the cauliflower is cooked all the way through. Stir at regular intervals to prevent burning.

5. Serve the hot curry ladled over steamed jasmine rice, and garnished with coriander leaves, snap peas, and cashews, and the lime wedges on the side.

# TUSCAN FARRO SOUP

COOK TIME: 45-50 MINS | MAKES: 4 SERVINGS

## INGREDIENTS:

- 3 tbsp. extra-virgin avocado oil
- 1 large shallot, chopped
- 1 1/2 tsp. Himalayan salt (divided)
- 3 celery stalks, chopped into 1/4-inch pieces
- 4 medium carrots, chopped into 1/4-inch half moons
- 2 tsp. crushed garlic
- 14 oz. canned diced tomatoes
- 1/4 tsp. cayenne pepper
- 1/4 tsp. freshly ground black pepper
- 2 tsp. fresh rosemary, chopped
- 1/2 cup farro
- 5 cups vegetable stock
- 15.5 oz. canned cannellini beans, rinsed and drained
- 4 cups kale leaves

## DIRECTIONS:

1. Heat the oil over medium-high heat in a large pot. When the oil is nice and hot, fry the shallots with 1/4 teaspoon salt for 5-6 minutes, or until the shallots are nicely caramelized. Add the celery and carrots, stirring and frying for an additional 5-6 minutes, or until the carrots soften slightly. Stir in the garlic, and allow the flavors to meld for 2 minutes. Add the tomatoes and stir for 2 minutes.

2. Add the remaining salt, the cayenne pepper, black pepper, rosemary, farro, and vegetable stock. Once the soup begins to boil, reduce the heat to maintain a gentle simmer for 25 minutes with the lid partially covering the pot, or until the farro is cooked.

3. Add the beans and kale leaves, and simmer the soup for an additional 2 minutes until the beans are heated through and the kale has wilted. Taste the soup, and adjust the seasoning as desired.

4. Ladle the soup into bowls, and serve hot, garnished with extra black pepper if desired.

# ROBUST CHICKPEA & NOODLE SOUP

COOK TIME: 30 MINS | MAKES: 6 SERVINGS

## INGREDIENTS:

- 2 tbsp. extra-virgin olive oil
- 1 shallot, finely chopped
- 2 celery stalks, sliced into 1/4-inch pieces
- 3 carrots, sliced into 1/4-inch thick pieces
- Freshly ground black pepper
- 2 whole bay leaves
- 2 tsp. fresh thyme, minced
- 3 tbsp. nutritional yeast
- 15 oz. canned chickpeas, rinsed and drained
- 6 cups vegetable stock
- 1/2 cup ditalini pasta
- 2 tbsp. fresh parsley, minced
- Himalayan salt

## DIRECTIONS:

1. In a large pot over medium heat, heat the olive oil. When the oil is nice and hot, fry the shallots, celery, and carrots with 1/4 teaspoon pepper for 5-7 minutes, or until the carrots soften. Add the bay leaves, thyme, and nutritional yeast, allowing the flavors to meld for 30 seconds while stirring.

2. Add the chickpeas and stock, stirring until the soup begins to boil. Lower the heat to maintain a gentle simmer for 1o minutes with the lid partially covering the pot.

3. Discard the bay leaves. Bring the heat back up to medium-high, and stir in the pasta. Cook for 10 minutes until the pasta is al dente.

4. Remove the pot from the heat, and stir in the fresh parsley leaves. Add salt and pepper if required.

5. Ladle the soup into bowls, and serve hot.

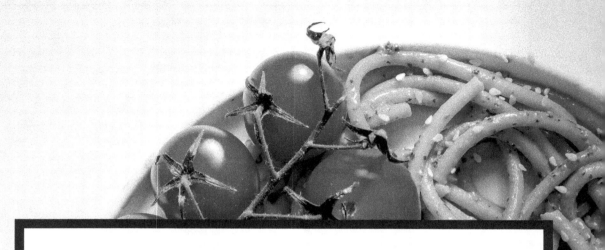

# NOODLES & PASTA

# CRISPY GRILLED EGGPLANT & SOBA NOODLES

COOK TIME: 30 MINS | MAKES: 4 SERVINGS

## INGREDIENTS:

**Marinade:**
- 2 tsp. crushed garlic
- 1 tbsp. pure maple syrup
- 2 tbsp. toasted sesame oil
- 1/4 cup tamari
- 1/4 cup filtered water
- 1/2 cup rice vinegar
- 1 lb. eggplant, sliced into 1/4-inch rounds
- Olive oil

**Soba noodles:**
- 8 oz. uncooked soba noodles
- 1 tbsp. rice vinegar
- 1 tbsp. toasted sesame oil
- 3 tbsp. filtered water
- 1/2 cup fresh basil leaves, roughly chopped
- 1 1/2 tbsp. lightly toasted sesame seeds

## DIRECTIONS:

1. In a shallow dish, whisk together the garlic, maple syrup, sesame oil, tamari, filtered water, and rice vinegar. Submerge the eggplant rounds in the marinade. Cover the bowl with cling wrap, and chill for a minimum of 15 minutes, or up to 1 hour.

2. Meanwhile, prepare the soba noodles according to the package instructions. Strain the noodles in a colander set over the sink, and rinse with cool water. Place the noodles in a large mixing bowl, and gently toss with the rice vinegar and toasted sesame oil.

3. Set a grill pan to preheat on high, and grease the pan with olive oil. When the pan is nice and hot, fry the marinated eggplant rounds for 2-3 minutes per side, or until the rounds are evenly toasted. Reserve the leftover marinade. If it looks like the rounds are drying out, use a basting brush to coat them with marinade while grilling.

4. Place the grilled rounds on a plate, and chop them into 1/2-inch squares.

5. In a medium-sized mixing bowl, whisk 1/2 cup of the eggplant marinade with 3 tablespoons filtered water. Pour the mixture over the soba noodles, and gently toss to combine.

6. Add the eggplant squares and basil leaves, and toss to combine.

7. Garnish the bowl with toasted sesame seeds, and serve hot or cold.

# SUPER SAUCY GARLIC ZITI

COOK TIME: 45 MINS | MAKES: 8-10 SERVINGS

## INGREDIENTS:

- 1/4 cup extra-virgin olive oil
- 1/2 shallot, roughly chopped
- 12 garlic cloves, halved
- 24 oz. canned marinara sauce
- 1/4 tsp. freshly ground black pepper
- 1/4 tsp. cayenne pepper (extra for garnish)
- 1/2 tsp. kosher salt
- 2 cups vegan mozzarella shreds (divided)
- 1 lb. cooked ziti pasta
- Italian seasoning

## DIRECTIONS:

1. Set the oven to preheat to 375°F, with the wire rack in the center of the oven.

2. Add the olive oil to a large casserole dish, and toss with the shallots and garlic cloves. Place the dish in the oven for 16 minutes, or until the shallots are soft and the garlic is nicely roasted.

3. Add the marinara sauce, black pepper, cayenne pepper, salt, 1 1/2 cups mozzarella, and the cooked pasta to the baking dish, and stir until all the ingredients are properly incorporated.

4. Sprinkle the top of the sauce with Italian seasoning, and add the remaining mozzarella. Garnish with a small sprinkling of extra cayenne pepper if desired.

5. Return the dish to the oven for 30 minutes, until the mozzarella is bubbling and lightly toasted.

6. Serve hot, and enjoy.

# DECADENT COCONUT PAD THAI

COOK TIME: 20-25 MINS | MAKES: 6 SERVINGS

## INGREDIENTS:

**Coconut sauce:**
- 3/4 cup canned coconut milk
- 1/4 tsp. kosher salt
- 1/2 tsp. garlic powder
- 1/2 tsp. ground ginger
- 1 tbsp. sriracha sauce
- 1/2 cup crunchy peanut butter
- 1 tbsp. toasted sesame oil
- 1 tbsp. seasoned rice vinegar
- 1/2 lime, juiced
- 2 tbsp. tamari
- 1/4 cup agave syrup

**Noodles:**
- 14 oz. thin rice noodles
- 2 tbsp. toasted sesame oil (divided)
- 1 cup carrots, shredded
- 1 red bell pepper, thinly sliced
- 1 bunch spring onions, sliced into 2-inch strips

**Toppings:**
- Fresh coriander leaves, chopped (for garnish)
- Lime wedges (for garnish)
- Crushed peanuts (for garnish)
- Fresh bean sprouts (for garnish)

## DIRECTIONS:

1. Shake the can of coconut milk well, then open it and place 3/4 cup into a high-powered food processor. Add in the salt, garlic powder, ginger, sriracha sauce, peanut butter, sesame oil, rice vinegar, lime juice, tamari, and agave syrup, and blend on high until you have a smooth paste.

2. Prepare the noodles according to package instructions, and drain in a colander set over the sink. Rinse with cool water. Add the noodles to a large mixing bowl, and toss with half of the toasted sesame oil.

3. In the same pot over medium heat, heat the remaining sesame oil. When the oil is nice and hot, fry the carrots and bell peppers for 2-4 minutes until they soften. Stir in the spring onions for 1 minute, or until just softened.

4. Toss in the coconut sauce and the cooked noodles, and stir until all the ingredients are properly combined.

5. Spoon the noodles into serving bowls, and garnish with your choice of toppings.

**Quick Tip:**
The coconut sauce tends to thicken when it cools. Add a few tablespoons of filtered water when reheating the noodles to loosen the sauce.

# NUTTY PHILIPPINES-STYLE CASHEW PASTA

COOK TIME: 20 MINS | MAKES: 3 SERVINGS

## INGREDIENTS:

**Sauce:**
- 1/4 tsp. kosher salt
- 1 1/2 tsp. cayenne pepper
- 2 tbsp. toasted sesame oil
- 2 1/2 tbsp. organic dark brown sugar
- 1 tbsp. dry sherry
- 3/4 cup filtered water, plus 2 tbsp. (divided)
- 2 1/2 tbsp. hoisin sauce
- 3 tbsp. kikkoman soy sauce
- 1 tbsp. corn flour

**Pasta:**
- 1/2 lb. linguini pasta
- 2 tbsp. toasted sesame oil
- 1/4 cup spring onions, chopped (extra for garnish)
- 1 small shallot, diced
- 3 tsp. crushed garlic
- 7 oz. button mushrooms, sliced
- 1/4 cup lightly toasted cashews

## DIRECTIONS:

1. In a small glass bowl, whisk together the salt, cayenne pepper, sesame oil, brown sugar, sherry, 3/4 cup water, hoisin sauce, and soy sauce, until all the sugar granules have dissolved.

2. In a separate glass bowl, mix together the remaining water and corn flour.

3. Fill a medium-sized pot with water, and bring to a boil over high heat. Cook the pasta according to package instructions until almost done. You don't want to fully cook the pasta at this point, as it will continue to cook while you prepare the rest of the dish. Strain the pasta, and set aside.

4. In a large frying pan over medium-high heat, heat the toasted sesame oil. When the oil is nice and hot, fry the spring onions, shallots, and garlic for 1 minute, allowing the flavors to meld. Add the mushrooms, and stir for 3 minutes until they darken in color. Give the bowl of sauce a good whisk before gradually stirring it into the pan.

5. Once the sauce begins to boil, reduce the heat to medium, and slowly whisk in the corn flour mixture until the sauce begins to thicken.

6. Stir in the pasta, and allow to simmer for 2-3 minutes, or until al dente.

7. Add the extra spring onions and the cashews, gently stirring to combine.

8. Plate the pasta, and serve.

# VEGAN-STYLE TOFU PAD THAI

COOK TIME: 25 MINS | MAKES: 4 SERVINGS

## INGREDIENTS:

**Pad Thai Sauce:**
- 3 tbsp. rice vinegar
- 3 tbsp. tomato paste
- 3 tbsp. organic dark brown sugar
- 3 tbsp. filtered water
- 1/4 cup kikkoman soy sauce
- 1/4 cup freshly squeezed lime juice

**Pasta:**
- 14 oz. rice noodles
- 2 tsp. toasted sesame oil
- 1/3 cup yellow onions, sliced

- 1 medium broccoli head, chopped into small florets
- 4 tsp. crushed garlic
- 3 oz. dry-fried tofu
- 1/4 cup fresh coriander leaves, chopped
- 1 cup spring onions, sliced

**Garnish:**
- 1 cup grated carrots
- 1 cup grated cabbage
- 1 cup bean sprouts
- Peanuts, roughly chopped
- Lime wedges

## DIRECTIONS:

1. In a small glass bowl, whisk together the vinegar, tomato paste, brown sugar, water, soy sauce, and lime juice, until all the sugar granules have dissolved. Set aside.

2. Cook the rice noodles according to package instructions, and rinse with cool water after straining.

3. In a large wok over medium heat, heat the toasted sesame oil. When the oil is nice and hot, fry the onions for 2 minutes, or until the edges become translucent. Add the broccoli, and fry for another 2 minutes until the florets just begin to soften. Stir in the garlic, and allow the flavors to meld for 30 seconds.

4. Add the rinsed noodles and 1/3 cup of the soy sauce mixture, gently tossing until the noodles are evenly coated. Add the dry-fried tofu, tossing for 30-60 seconds until properly combined. Toss in the coriander leaves and spring onions. Add sauce until the dish is saucy enough for you – the tofu will absorb some of the sauce as you cook.

5. Plate the noodles, and serve hot, garnished with carrots, cabbage, bean sprouts, peanuts, and lime wedges.

# SWEET & SAVORY CHAR KWAY TEOW

COOK TIME: 20 MINS | MAKES: 2 SERVINGS

## INGREDIENTS:

**Noodles:**
- 4.5 oz. dried, flat white rice noodles
- 7 oz. extra-firm tempeh
- 4 tbsp. toasted sesame oil (divided)
- 1 tbsp. sweet soy sauce
- 3 tsp. crushed garlic
- 1/4 cup shallots, sliced
- 1/8 tsp. Himalayan salt

- 1 tsp. ground turmeric
- 1 oz. fresh chives, chopped
- 2 cups bean sprouts

**Sauce:**
- 1 tsp. sriracha sauce
- 1 1/2 tbsp. sweet soy sauce
- 1 1/2 tsp. vegan oyster sauce
- 1 tbsp. kikkoman soy sauce

## DIRECTIONS:

1. Submerge the noodles in a bowl of boiling water, and stir a few times. Let the noodles soak for 8-10 minutes, until they gain color and are no longer see-through. Strain the noodles, and set aside.

2. Place the tempeh on a large, rimmed baking sheet between 2 stacks of paper towels, 4 at the bottom and 4 on top. Use a heavy stack of books or a large pot to press the tempeh down for at least 10 minutes. Discard the paper towels when the tempeh is properly pressed. Divide the tempeh into 2 equal portions. Crumble and mash one portion into a large bowl, and slice the second portion into strips 1/2-inch thick.

3. In a small glass bowl, whisk together the sriracha sauce, sweet soy sauce, vegan oyster sauce, and soy sauce. Set aside.

4. In a large frying pan over high heat, heat two tablespoons of the toasted sesame oil. When the oil is nice and hot, fry the tempeh strips for 3-4 minutes per side until golden and crispy on all sides. Add the sweet soy sauce, and stir to combine. Continue to cook the tempeh until it just begins to char around the edges.

5. Push the tempeh to the side of the pan, and add the remaining toasted sesame oil. When the oil is sizzling, add the garlic and shallots, frying for 1 minute. Add the noodles to the pan, and pour the sauce over everything. Gently toss the noodles for 2-3 minutes, until evenly coated in the sauce and heated through.

6. Raise the heat to medium-high, and push the noodles to the side of the pan. Scrape the mashed tempeh into the pan, and sprinkle with salt and turmeric. Continue to stir and fry the tempeh until it begins to resemble scrambled eggs.

7. Add the chives and bean sprouts, stirring to combine. Crank the heat up to high, and toss everything together for 2-3 minutes until properly combined. The bean sprouts should be properly cooked.

8. Plate the noodles, and serve immediately.

# SPICY ASIAN-STYLE EGGPLANT NOODLES

COOK TIME: 20 MINS | MAKES: 2 SERVINGS

## INGREDIENTS:

- 12 oz. Chinese eggplant
- 1 tsp. coarse sea salt

**Sauce:**
- 1/2 cup vegetable stock, room temperature
- 2 tbsp. organic dark brown sugar
- 1 tbsp. corn flour
- 1 tbsp. dry sherry
- 1 tbsp. Chinese black vinegar
- 1 tbsp. kikkoman soy sauce

**Noodles:**
- 1/4 cup dried textured vegetable protein

- 5 oz. dried linguine noodles
- 2 tsp. extra-virgin olive oil

**Stir-Fry:**
- 3 tbsp. toasted sesame oil
- 1 1/2 tsp. freshly grated ginger
- 3 tsp. crushed garlic
- 1 small shallot, diced
- 2 tbsp. chili broad bean paste
- 1 small red bell pepper, seeded and diced
- Kosher salt
- Spring onions, chopped (for garnish)

## DIRECTIONS:

1. Place the eggplants on a wooden chopping board, and slice them into sticks about 3-inches long and 1-inch thick. Submerge the eggplant sticks in a bowl of room temperature water, and add 1 teaspoon of coarse sea salt. Allow the eggplant to soak for at least 10 minutes.

2. In a small glass bowl, whisk together the vegetable stock, sugar, corn flour, sherry, black vinegar, and soy sauce. Set aside.

3. Place a small strainer over a large bowl, and place the vegetable protein in it. Submerge it in boiling water, and soak for 5 minutes, or until the protein is no longer dry.

4. While the protein is soaking, bring a large pot of water to a rolling boil over high heat. Cook the linguine until just about done – you don't want to cook the noodles all the way at this stage. Strain the noodles, and rinse with cool water, then transfer the rinsed noodles to two separate bowls in equal amounts. Add 1 teaspoon of olive oil to each bowl, and toss to coat.

5. In a large wok, heat the toasted sesame oil. When the oil is nice and hot, fry the ginger, garlic, and shallots for 1-2 minutes, allowing the flavors to meld. Raise the heat to high, and stir in the chili paste and bell peppers for 1-2 minutes, or until the peppers become tender.

6. Strain the water from the eggplant sticks and add them to the pan, frying for 6 minutes over medium-high heat until they soften.

7. Strain the water from the vegetable proteins and add them to the pan, tossing to combine.

8. Lower the heat to medium. Whisk the sauce once more to ensure that there are no clumps, before gradually whisking it into the pan. Taste, and add additional salt if required. Crank the heat back up to medium-high, and stir for 2 minutes, or until the sauce begins to thicken.

9. Pour the sauce over the two bowls of noodles, and stir to combine. Serve hot, garnished with spring onions, and enjoy!

# FAUX MEATBALLS

COOK TIME: 40 -50 MINS | MAKES: 4 SERVINGS

## INGREDIENTS:

- 8 oz. medium button mushrooms, quartered
- 1 medium eggplant, peeled and cut into 1/2-inch cubes
- 1/4 tsp. cayenne pepper
- 1/4 tsp. ground white pepper
- 1 tsp. Himalayan salt (divided)
- 1/4 cup extra-virgin olive oil
- 3 tsp. crushed garlic
- 1 tsp. dried oregano
- 1/2 cup fresh parsley, chopped (more for garnish)
- 15.5 oz. canned chickpeas, drained and rinsed
- 3/4 cup panko breadcrumbs
- Canned marinara sauce

## DIRECTIONS:

1. Set the oven to preheat to 425°F, with the wire rack in the center of the oven.

2. In a large mixing bowl, toss the mushrooms and eggplant with the cayenne pepper, white pepper, 1/2 teaspoon salt, olive oil, and garlic, until the mushrooms and eggplant are evenly coated. Fan the seasoned vegetables out on a large, rimmed baking tray in a single layer, and bake for 15 minutes before flipping, and baking for an additional 15-20 minutes. The vegetables should be fork-tender. Allow to cool on the counter for a few minutes.

3. Transfer the slightly cooled vegetables to a high-powered food processor, along with the remaining salt, oregano, parsley, and chickpeas. Blend on high until you have a smooth paste. Scrape the paste into a medium-sized mixing bowl, and stir in the breadcrumbs.

4. Cover a clean, large, rimmed baking tray with grease-proof paper, and set aside.

5. Use clean hands to shape the mixture into 22 balls of roughly the same size. Arrange the balls on the prepared baking tray.

6. Place the meatballs in the oven for 20-25 minutes, or until they are cooked all the way through.

7. Toss the meatballs in the marinara sauce and serve as is, garnished with extra parsley, or on a bed of cooked spaghetti.

**Quick Tip:**
If you want the meatballs to maintain their crispy texture, toss them in the marinara sauce just before serving.

# BASIL & TOMATO MACARONI

COOK TIME: 20-30 MINS | MAKES: 4-6 SERVINGS

## INGREDIENTS:

- Flaky sea salt
- 1 lb. elbow noodles
- 1/4 cup extra-virgin olive oil
- 4 tsp. crushed garlic
- 1 tbsp. tomato paste
- 1/4 tsp. brown sugar
- 1/4 tsp. cayenne pepper
- 1/4 tsp. freshly ground black pepper
- 1 fresh basil sprig (extra leaves for garnish)
- 1\2 cup filtered water
- 7 cups cherry tomatoes

## DIRECTIONS:

1. Bring a large pot of salted water to a rolling boil over medium-high heat, and cook the elbow noodles according to package instructions. Drain the noodles in a colander set over the sink, and rinse with cool water.

2. Heat the oil in a large pot over medium heat. When the oil is nice and hot, fry the garlic for 1-2 minutes until fragrant. Stir in the tomato paste for 30 seconds until it begins to brown.

3. Add 1 teaspoon salt, the sugar, cayenne pepper, black pepper, basil sprig, water, and tomatoes, stirring to combine. Simmer covered for 8-10 minutes, or until the tomatoes burst open. Stir the sauce every few minutes to prevent burning. When the tomatoes have burst open, remove the lid and simmer uncovered for 3-5 minutes until the sauce begins to thicken.

4. Add the pasta, and stir until it is coated and heated through.

5. Serve hot, garnished with extra basil leaves.

# VODKA-SOAKED MOCK LOBSTER PASTA

COOK TIME: 35-40 MINS | MAKES: 6 SERVINGS

## INGREDIENTS:

- 1 cup dried lobster mushrooms
- Flaky sea salt
- 1 lb. elbow noodles
- 5 tbsp. extra virgin olive oil (divided)
- 1 shallot, finely diced
- 2 tsp. crushed garlic
- 6 oz. canned tomato paste
- 1/4 tsp. cayenne pepper

- 1/2 cup vodka
- Freshly ground black pepper
- 1/4 cup dry white wine
- 2 tbsp. nutritional yeast
- 1 cup cashew heavy cream
- 1/4 cup fresh basil leaves, thinly sliced
- 1/2 cup panko bread crumbs

## DIRECTIONS:

1. Submerge the lobster mushrooms in a bowl of boiling water for 30 minutes, or until they are rehydrated. Drain the mushrooms in a colander set over the sink, then chop them into 1/2-inch pieces. Set aside in a bowl.

2. Bring a large pot of salted water to a rolling boil over medium heat. When the water begins to boil, add the noodles, and cook according to package instructions until the desired level of doneness. Remove two cups of water from the pot, and set aside before draining the pasta. Place the pasta in a large bowl, and toss with 1 tablespoon of olive oil.

3. Heat 3 tablespoons of olive oil in a large pot over medium heat. When the oil is nice and hot, add the shallots and fry for 8-10 minutes, or until nicely caramelized. Stir in the garlic, allowing the flavors to meld for 30 seconds.

4. Add the cayenne pepper and tomato paste, stirring for 2 minutes until the paste begins to brown. Pour the vodka into the pot, and scrape the bottom with a wooden spoon to deglaze. Taste the sauce, and season with extra salt and freshly ground black pepper as desired. Add one cup of the reserved pasta water, and stir for 3-5 minutes until at least half of the liquid has evaporated. Turn off the heat, and let the pot stand for a few minutes while you prepare the rest of the dish.

5. Heat the remaining oil in a small frying pan over medium-high heat. When the oil is nice and hot, fry the rehydrated mushrooms for 2 minutes, or until they are nicely browned. Add a pinch of salt, and stir. Stir in the wine for 1-2 minutes, or until it has cooked away by at least half. Transfer the pan to a wooden chopping board, and set aside.

6. Turn the heat back on to medium under the pot of tomato sauce. Add the nutritional yeast, cashew cream, and final cup of reserved pasta water, stirring to combine. When the sauce is properly incorporated, scrape the mushrooms into the pot, and add the cooked pasta. Stir until everything is properly combined. Turn off the heat when the pasta is heated all the way through.

7. Scoop the pasta into bowls and serve hot, garnished with fresh basil leaves and panko bread crumbs.

# DECADENT BROCCOLI FARFALLE PASTA

COOK TIME: 10-15 MINS | MAKES: 10-12 SERVINGS

## INGREDIENTS:

- 1/4 tsp. ground white pepper
- 1/2 tsp. dried rosemary
- 3 tbsp. nutritional yeast
- 1/2 lemon, juiced
- 2 tsp. Himalayan salt
- 1 tsp. onion powder
- 1 tsp. garlic powder
- 2 cups filtered water
- 1 1/2 cups raw cashews, soaked or boiled until soft
- 1 lb. farfalle pasta
- 1 cup sun-dried tomatoes, roughly chopped
- 1 head broccoli, sliced into bite-sized florets

## DIRECTIONS:

1. In a high-powered food processor, pulse the pepper, rosemary, yeast, lemon juice, salt, onion powder, garlic powder, filtered water, and cashews on high until you have a smooth paste.

2. Heat a large pot of salted water over medium heat. When the water is boiling, add the pasta, and cook according to package instructions until al dente. Add the sundried tomatoes and broccoli florets to the pot of pasta for the final two minutes of cooking.

3. Drain the pasta and vegetables in a colander set over the sink. Return the pasta and veg to the pot, and stir in the sauce.

4. Scoop the pasta into bowls, and serve hot.

**Quick Tip:**
This pasta sauce can be prepared in advance, and refrigerated in an airtight container for no more than 7 days.

# VEGAN-STYLE SOY-BRAISED NOODLES

COOK TIME: 20 MINS | MAKES: 4 SERVINGS

## INGREDIENTS:

- 2 cups boiling water
- 1 oz. dried shiitake mushrooms
- Kosher salt
- 6.5 oz. dried mein noodles
- 3 tbsp. extra-virgin olive oil
- 3 tsp. crushed garlic
- 1 medium shallot, chopped
- 3 cups cabbage, chopped

- 1 tbsp. dry sherry
- 1/8 tsp. freshly ground black pepper
- 1 tbsp. organic dark brown sugar
- 2 tbsp. kikkoman soy sauce (divided)
- 1 1/2 tbsp. dark soy sauce
- 2 tbsp. filtered water, room temperature
- 1 tbsp. corn flour
- 1/4 cup fresh chives, chopped

## DIRECTIONS:

1. Pour the boiling water into a large mixing bowl, and submerge the mushrooms for 10-15 minutes until they are rehydrated. Transfer the mushrooms to a wooden chopping board, and reserve the boiled water. Chop the mushrooms into 1/2-inch pieces.

2. Bring a medium pot of salted water to a rolling boil over medium heat. When the water is boiling, add the noodles, and cook according to package instructions until they are just under done. The noodles will continue to cook later on in the cooking process. Drain the noodles in a colander set over the sink.

3. Heat the oil in a large frying pan over medium-high heat. When the oil is nice and hot, fry the garlic and shallots for 1 minute until fragrant. Add the chopped shiitake mushrooms and cabbage, and fry undisturbed for 2 minutes until just beginning to brown. Stir, and brown the opposite sides of the mushrooms. Crank the heat up to high and stir in the sherry, simmering until the liquid cooks away.

4. Stir in the pepper, reserved mushroom water, sugar, 1 tablespoon soy sauce, and dark brown soy sauce. Bring the sauce to a boil, and stir for 3-4 minutes. Lower the heat to maintain a gentle simmer, and add the noodles, simmering for 2 minutes.

5. In a small glass bowl, whisk the filtered water and corn flour together until you have a lump-free paste. Gradually whisk the paste into the sauce, and stir for a few minutes until the sauce starts to thicken. Taste, and adjust the seasoning as needed, with extra soy sauce if desired. Turn off the heat, and stir in the chives.

6. Plate the noodles, and serve.

# COMFORT VEGAN MAC & CHEESE

COOK TIME: 40-45 MINS | MAKES: 10-12 SERVINGS

## INGREDIENTS:

**Sauce:**
- 1 1/2 tsp. onion powder
- 1 1/2 tsp. garlic powder
- 1 1/2 tsp. kosher salt
- 1/2 lemon, juiced
- 1 tbsp. agave syrup
- 1 tbsp. kikkoman soy sauce
- 1 tbsp. French mustard
- 3 cups filtered water
- 2 tbsp. white miso paste
- 1/4 cup nutritional yeast
- 1/2 cup raw cashews, boiled or soaked until soft
- 1 1/2 cups canned pumpkin purée

**Mac:**
- Baking spray
- Flaky sea salt
- 1 lb. elbow macaroni pasta
- 1/2 cup vegan cheddar cheese
- 1/2 cup panko bread crumbs
- 2 tbsp. vegan butter, melted
- 1-2 tsp. sweet smoked paprika

## DIRECTIONS:

1. In a high-powered food processor, process the onion powder, garlic powder, salt, lemon juice, agave syrup, soy sauce, mustard, water, miso paste, yeast, cashews, and pumpkin purée on high until you have a smooth and creamy paste.

2. Set the oven to preheat to 350°F, with the wire rack in the center of the oven, and coat a large casserole dish with baking spray.

3. Bring a large pot of salted water to a rolling boil over medium heat. Add the pasta, and cook according to package instructions. Drain the pasta in a colander set over the sink. Return the pasta to the pot, and mix in the sauce from the food processor. Add the cheese, and mix to combine.

4. Scrape the pasta into the prepared casserole dish.

5. In a medium-sized bowl, combine the bread crumbs and vegan butter. Strew the crumb mixture evenly over the macaroni. Garnish the crumbs with paprika.

6. Place the dish in the oven for 30-35 minutes, or until the top is nicely browned.

7. Scoop the pasta onto plates, and serve warm.

# TANGY VEGAN YAKISOBA

COOK TIME: 15 MINS | MAKES: 2 SERVINGS

## INGREDIENTS:

**Sauce:**
- 1/8 tsp. ground white pepper
- 2 tbsp. vegan oyster sauce
- 2 tbsp. organic dark brown sugar
- 2 tbsp. tomato ketchup
- 2 tsp. rice vinegar
- 1 1/2 tbsp. kikkoman soy sauce

**Noodles:**
- 10 oz. cooked or raw yakisoba noodles
- 2 tbsp. toasted sesame oil
- 1 small shallot, sliced
- 1 spring onion, chopped (more for garnish)
- Flaky sea salt
- 1 small red bell pepper, seeded and diced
- 6 fresh shiitake mushrooms
- 8 cabbage leaves, chopped
- 1 small carrot, thinly sliced

## DIRECTIONS:

1. In a small glass bowl, whisk together the pepper, oyster sauce, sugar, ketchup, rice vinegar, and soy sauce. Taste the sauce, and adjust the seasoning as desired.

2. Place the cooked noodles in a colander set over the sink, and rinse with warm water. If preparing fresh noodles, simply cook by following the directions on the packaging, then rinse with warm water.

3. Heat the oil in a large frying pan over medium-high heat. When the oil is nice and hot, fry the shallots and spring onions for 2 minutes, allowing the flavors to meld.

4. Add a pinch of salt to the pan, along with the bell pepper, mushrooms, cabbage, and carrot. Cook the vegetables over medium-high for 3-4 minutes, until the carrots just begin to soften.

5. Stir in the noodles, and gradually pour in the sauce while stirring. Continue to stir for 2-3 minutes, or until the liquid has mostly evaporated.

6. Transfer the noodles to serving bowls and serve immediately, garnished with extra spring onions.

# QUICK & EASY PASTA FAGIOLI

COOK TIME: 15-20 MINS | MAKE: 4 SERVINGS

## INGREDIENTS:

- 4 cups vegetable stock
- 2 garlic cloves, halved
- 1 cup ditalini pasta
- 15 oz. canned white kidney beans, rinsed and drained
- 2 cups grape tomatoes, halved
- 1/2 tsp. kosher salt (more if needed)
- 1 tbsp. tomato paste
- Fresh basil leaves (for garnish)
- Extra-virgin olive oil (for garnish)

## DIRECTIONS:

1. In a large pot over medium-high heat, bring the vegetable stock and garlic to a boil. Once the stock is boiling, reduce the heat to maintain a gentle simmer for 3 minutes.

2. Add the pasta, kidney beans, and grape tomatoes, and cook for 8-10 minutes, or until the ditalini reaches the desired level of doneness.

3. Stir in the salt and tomato paste. Taste the soup, and adjust the seasoning as needed. Remove and discard the garlic halves.

4. Ladle the soup into bowls, and serve hot, garnished with fresh basil leaves and a drizzle of olive oil.

# DESSERTS

# LIGHT & FLUFFY COCONUTTY CUPCAKES

COOK TIME: 25 MINS | MAKES: 9 SERVINGS

## INGREDIENTS:

- 1/2 tsp. distilled white vinegar
- 3/4 cup almond milk, room temperature
- 1/2 cup unsweetened coconut shreds
- 1/4 tsp. kosher salt
- 1/8 tsp. baking soda
- 1/4 tsp. baking powder
- 1 cup all-purpose flour
- 1/2 tsp. pure vanilla essence
- 1/4 cup full-fat coconut milk
- 5 tbsp. organic dark brown sugar
- 3 tbsp. pure coconut oil, melted
- Lightly toasted coconut chips (for garnish)

## DIRECTIONS:

1. Set the oven to preheat to 350°F, with the wire rack in the center of the oven, and line 9 cups of a muffin tin with cupcake holders.

2. In a large mixing bowl, whisk together the vinegar and almond milk. Allow the bowl to stand on the counter for 5-10 minutes until the milk curdles.

3. In a separate mixing bowl, whisk together the coconut shreds, salt, baking soda, baking powder, and all-purpose flour until properly combined with no lumps.

4. To the bowl of curdled almond milk, add the vanilla, coconut milk, sugar, and coconut oil, whisking to combine.

5. Create a hole in the center of the flour mixture, and pour in the almond milk mixture. Use a wooden spoon to gently combine the mixture until all of the dry ingredients have been incorporated. Do not overmix the batter – a few lumps won't hurt this recipe.

6. Divide the batter into the cupcake liners in the tin – about 2 heaped tablespoons per liner.

7. Bake in the oven for 20-25 minutes, or until an inserted skewer comes out clean. Remove the cupcakes from the tin, and allow them to cool on a wire rack before garnishing with the toasted coconut chips and serving.

**Quick Tip:**
The cupcakes can be kept at room temperature for 2 days, or refrigerated in an airtight container for no more than 7 days.

# SMOOTH & SILKY CHOCOLATE PUDDING

COOK TIME: 7-10 MINS | MAKES: 4 SERVINGS

## INGREDIENTS:

- 1/4 tsp. kosher salt
- 3 tbsp. corn flour
- 1/4 cup unsweetened cocoa powder
- 6 tbsp. organic brown sugar
- 2 cups almond milk
- 1/2 tsp. pure vanilla essence
- 1/3 cup vegan dark chocolate chips
- 1/4 tsp. ground nutmeg

## DIRECTIONS:

1. Place the salt, corn flour, cocoa powder, and sugar in a small pot, and whisk until the ingredients are properly combined. Gradually whisk in half of the almond milk until you have a smooth paste. Then whisk in the rest.

2. With the pot over medium heat, use a wooden spoon to gently stir the mixture for 4-5 minutes. Once the pudding begins to simmer, stir for another 2-3 minutes until it is thick enough to coat the back of a wooden spoon.

3. Transfer the pot to a wooden chopping board, and whisk in the vanilla essence, chocolate chips, and nutmeg.

4. Scoop the pudding into 4 serving bowls in equal amounts, and tightly seal the bowls with cling wrap. Chill for a minimum of 2 hours, or until the pudding is completely set.

5. Serve after a delicious vegan dinner.

# FRUITY TAPIOCA PUDDING

COOK TIME: 10-15 MINS | MAKES: 4 SERVINGS

## INGREDIENTS:

- 2 cups filtered water
- 1/2 cup tapioca pearls
- 1/2 tsp. pure vanilla essence
- Kosher salt
- 1 cup unsweetened almond milk
- 3 cups peach juice
- 1 tbsp. pure maple syrup
- 2 tbsp. freshly squeezed lemon juice
- Ground cinnamon (for garnish)
- Blueberries (for garnish)

## DIRECTIONS:

1. Place the filtered water in a large bowl, and stir in the tapioca pearls. Allow to soak for 6-16 hours. Overnight is preferable, but do not exceed 16 hours.

2. Strain the water from the tapioca, and add the soaked pearls to a medium-sized pot. Stir in the vanilla essence, a pinch of salt, the almond milk, and peach juice, and add the maple syrup if you like a sweeter pudding.

3. Stir over low heat for 8-10 minutes, keeping a close eye on the heat – you do not want the pudding to simmer or boil. Once the tapioca pearls become translucent, continue to stir just until the sauce thickens. Scrape the pudding into a serving bowl, and stir in the lemon juice. Seal with plastic wrap, and chill for 3-4 hours.

4. When you are ready to serve the pudding, whisk in some extra peach juice if the pudding is too thick for your liking. Spoon into bowls and serve, garnished with a sprinkling of cinnamon and blueberries.

# CRUNCHY RASPBERRY SHORTBREAD BARS

COOK TIME: 30-35 MINS | MAKES: 24 SERVINGS

## INGREDIENTS:

- Baking spray
- 1/2 tsp. kosher salt
- 2/3 cup organic dark brown sugar
- 2 1/2 cups all-purpose flour
- ¾ cups coconut oil (plus 2 tbsp.)
- 3 tbsp. filtered water
- 1/4 cup fine organic light brown sugar
- 1/2 cup lightly toasted pecans, finely chopped
- 1/2 cup old-fashioned rolled oats
- 1/4 tsp. ground nutmeg
- 1 tbsp. freshly squeezed lemon juice
- 3/4 cup fresh raspberries
- 3/4 cup raspberry jam

## DIRECTIONS:

1. Set the oven to preheat to 375°F, with the wire rack in the center of the oven. Line a large, square casserole dish with tin foil. The tinfoil should be pressed tightly against the dish with flaps hanging over the edges to serve as handles. Generously coat the foil with baking spray.

2. Place the salt, sugar, and flour in a high-powered food processor, and process on high until you have a fine powder. Add the coconut oil to the food processor, and drizzle the water over the top. Pulse on high until you have a mixture that resembles coarse sand. This process may take a few minutes. Set aside 1 1/4 cups of the flour mixture before scraping the rest into your prepared casserole dish. Use the bottom of a clean glass to press the mixture into the foil. Bake in the oven for 9 minutes, then rotate the dish and baking for an additional 9 minutes until the crust begins to brown.

3. Place the reserved flour mixture in a large mixing bowl, and whisk in the light brown sugar, pecans, oats, and nutmeg. Crumble and pinch the mixture until you have smallish chunks of varying sizes.

4. In a separate mixing bowl, mix together the jam, raspberries, and lemon juice. Use a fork to mash the raspberries, leaving a few small chunks for texture.

5. Spread the jam mixture evenly over the baked crust, and sprinkle with the crumble mixture. Bake in the oven for 12 minutes, then turn the dish and baking for an additional 12-15 minutes. The crumble topping should be a beautiful golden brown.

6. Allow the shortbread to cool for 2 hours before using the handles to lift the square out of the dish. Slice into bars, and serve.

# GREEN TEA MATCHA COOKIES

COOK TIME: 20 MINS | MAKES: 12 SERVINGS

## INGREDIENTS:

- 2 tbsp. filtered water, room temperature
- 1 tbsp. flaxseed meal
- 1-2 tsp. green matcha powder
- 1/4 tsp. kosher salt
- 1/2 tsp. baking soda

- 1 cup all-purpose flour
- 1/2 cup organic dark brown sugar
- 1/4 cup melted coconut oil
- 1/2 tsp. pure vanilla essence
- 2 tbsp. almond milk, room temperature

## DIRECTIONS:

1. In a small glass bowl, whisk together the filtered water and flaxseed meal. Cover the bowl, and chill until the mixture thickens – about 5 minutes.

2. Set the oven to preheat to 375°F, with the wire rack in the center of the oven, and line a large, rimmed baking sheet with greaseproof paper.

3. In a large mixing bowl, whisk together the matcha powder, salt, baking soda, and flour.

4. In a separate mixing bowl, whisk together the brown sugar and coconut oil until thoroughly combined. The mixture should be light and fluffy. Add the chilled flaxseed mixture, vanilla essence, and almond milk, whisking to combine.

5. Create a hole in the middle of the flour mixture, and scrape the wet ingredients into the center. Use a wooden spoon to gently combine the ingredients until there are no dry patches. You will have a relatively stiff cookie dough.

6. Use clean hands to form the dough into 12 balls of roughly the same size. Place the balls 3-inches apart on the prepared baking sheet, and use the back of a spoon to flatten into 2-inch thick discs.

7. If you prefer crispy cookies, bake in the oven for 15-16 minutes. Transfer to a wire rack, and allow to cool for 10 minutes.

8. For chewy cookies, bake in the oven for 12 minutes. Transfer to a wire rack, and allow to cool for 10 minutes.

9. Serve, and enjoy.

**Quick Tip:**
Any leftover cookies can be kept in an airtight container for 3 days at room temperature, or refrigerated in an airtight container for more than 7 days.

# FRUITY VEGAN LEMON CRUMBLE

COOK TIME: 45-50 MINS | MAKES: 6-8 SERVINGS

## INGREDIENTS:

**Crumble:**
- 1/4 tsp. flaky sea salt
- 1/4 tsp. ground nutmeg
- 1/3 cup organic dark brown sugar
- 1/3 cup granulated sugar
- 1/2 cup old-fashioned rolled oats
- 1 1/2 cups all-purpose flour, levelled
- 1/2 cup vegan butter

**Filling:**
- 1/8 tsp. kosher salt
- 1/2 tsp. ground cinnamon
- 1/2 tsp. finely grated lemon zest
- 3 tbsp. all-purpose flour
- 1/2 cup organic light brown sugar
- 7-8 cups fresh blueberries

## DIRECTIONS:

1. In a large mixing bowl, whisk together the salt, nutmeg, brown sugar, granulated sugar, oats, and flour. Add the vegan butter and work the mixture, either with your hands or with pastry knives, to cut and crumble the mixture into a crumbly topping. Cover and chill for 40 minutes, or place the bowl in the freezer for 20 minutes.

2. Set the oven to preheat to 375°F, with the wire rack in the center of the oven.

3. In a large mixing bowl, whisk together the salt, cinnamon, lemon zest, flour, light brown sugar, and blueberries until properly combined. Scrape the mixture into a large casserole dish in an even layer. There should be at least 1-inch of space left above the mixture.

4. Crumble the chilled topping over the blueberry mixture in an even layer. Place the dish on a large, rimmed baking tray, and bake in the oven for 45-50 minutes. The top should be a beautiful golden brown.

5. Allow to cool for a few minutes before serving.

**Quick Tip:**
This dish is best served and eaten on the same day, as it does not keep well.

# THE 4 C'S COOKIES

COOK TIME: 12-15 MINS | MAKES: 30 SERVINGS

## INGREDIENTS:

- 5 tbsp. filtered water
- 2 tbsp. flaxseed meal
- 1/2 tsp. kosher salt
- 1/4 tsp. ground nutmeg
- 1/4 tsp. ground cinnamon
- 1 tsp. baking soda
- 1/2 cup old-fashioned rolled oats
- 2 cups all-purpose flour
- 1/2 cup solid coconut oil
- 1 cup packed organic dark brown sugar
- 2 tsp. pure vanilla essence
- 12 oz. vegan dark chocolate chips
- 15.5 oz. canned chickpeas, rinsed and drained

## DIRECTIONS:

1. Set the oven to preheat to 350°F, with the wire rack in the center of the oven, and line 2 large baking sheets with greaseproof paper.

2. In a small glass bowl, whisk together the water and flaxseed meal. Cover the bowl, and set aside on the counter for 5-10 minutes until the mixture thickens.

3. In a large mixing bowl, whisk together the salt, nutmeg, cinnamon, baking soda, oats, and flour.

4. Place the coconut oil and brown sugar in a large mixing bowl, and use a hand mixer to beat until properly combined. Add the vanilla and thickened flaxseed mixture, and beat until you have a creamy batter. Add the chocolate chips and chickpeas, mixing to combine. With the mixer on the lowest setting, gradually beat in the flour mixture.

5. Use a tablespoon to scoop the batter onto the prepared baking sheets in 30 blobs, spaced 2-inches apart. Bake in the oven for 6 minutes, before rotating the sheets and baking for an additional 6-9 minutes until the cookies are a crispy brown around the edges.

6. Allow the cookies to cool for 5 minutes on the sheets before transferring them to a wire cooling rack. Allow to cool completely before serving.

# NUTTY, UPSIDE-DOWN CINNAMON BUNS

COOK TIME: 30-45 MINS | MAKES: 12 SERVINGS

## INGREDIENTS:

**Dough:**
- 3 tbsp. organic dark brown sugar
- 1/4 cup almond butter, melted
- 2 cups unsweetened almond milk, slightly warmed
- 2 1/4 tsp. active dry yeast
- 2 tsp. kosher salt
- 4 1/2 cups all-purpose flour (more if needed)

**Filling:**
- 2 tsp. ground cinnamon

- 1/2 cup organic dark brown sugar
- 1/4 cup almond butter, slightly softened
- Baking spray

**Topping:**
- 6 tbsp. pure maple syrup
- 3/4 cup almond butter, melted
- 1 cup organic light brown sugar
- 1 cup pecan halves, chopped

## DIRECTIONS:

1. In a large mixing bowl, whisk together the brown sugar, almond butter, and almond milk. Sprinkle the yeast over the surface of the milk mixture, and set the bowl aside on the counter for 3-5 minutes until the yeast blooms. Once the yeast has bloomed, sprinkle the salt over the yeast and add the flour. Use a wooden spoon to bring the ingredients together in a sticky dough. Cover the bowl with a slightly damp kitchen towel, and let the dough rise in a warm area, with no drafts, for 1-2 hours. The dough should double in size during this time.

2. Once the dough has risen, sprinkle 1/2 cup of flour onto a clean work surface, and knead until it is no longer sticky – about 3 minutes. Add a little more flour at a time if necessary. Gather the dough into a smooth ball, and tightly wrap with cling wrap. Let the dough ball rest on the counter for 10 minutes.

3. Roll the dough out, on a lightly-floured surface, into a rectangle of 15 x 18 inches. Sprinkle with more flour if the dough sticks to the rolling pin.

4. In a large mixing bowl, whisk together the cinnamon and dark brown sugar. Use a butter knife to spread the almond butter evenly over the dough rectangle. Sprinkle the cinnamon and sugar over the butter. Roll the rectangle up into a tight cylinder, and use a sharp knife to slice it into 12 circles of roughly the same size.

5. Generously coat a large casserole dish with baking spray.

6. In a clean mixing bowl, whisk together the pure maple syrup, almond butter, and light brown sugar. Fold in the chopped pecans. Scrape the mixture into the prepared baking dish in an even layer. Arrange the cinnamon rolls on top of the mixture in 4 rows of 3, evenly spaced apart. Cover the dish with cling wrap, and allow the buns to rise in a warm area, with no drafts, for 45-60 minutes until doubled in size.

7. Set the oven to preheat to 375°F, with the wire rack in the center of the oven.

8. Place the dish on a large, rimmed baking sheet, and bake in the oven for 15 minutes before turning, and baking for another 15-20 minutes. The buns are done when the tops are lightly browned and an inserted skewer comes out clean. If the buns look like they are browning too quickly, cover the dish with tin foil and continue to bake.

9. Place a serving platter on top of the dish, and carefully flip using oven mitts. Scrape any excess syrup and nuts from the dish onto the cinnamon rolls.

10. Allow the rolls to rest for 5 minutes before serving.

# CINNAMON OAT BROWNIES

COOK TIME: 45 MINS | MAKES: 9 SERVINGS

## INGREDIENTS:

- Baking spray
- 1 tsp. pure vanilla essence
- 2 tbsp. sunflower oil
- 1/2 cup unsweetened almond milk
- 3/4 cup organic dark brown sugar
- 2 tsp. ground cinnamon (divided)
- 1/4 tsp. ground nutmeg
- 1 tsp. kosher salt (divided)
- 1 1/2 tsp. baking powder
- 1 cup all-purpose flour
- 3/4 cup organic light brown sugar
- 1/4 cup old-fashioned rolled oats
- 2 tbsp. almond butter

## DIRECTIONS:

1. Set the oven to preheat to 350°F, with the wire rack in the center of the oven, and line a large, square baking dish with greaseproof paper. The paper should hang over the sides of the dish by a few inches to serve as handles. Generously coat the paper with baking spray.

2. In a large mixing bowl, whisk together the vanilla, oil, almond milk, dark brown sugar, half of the cinnamon, the nutmeg, half of the salt, the baking powder, and the flour. Scrape the batter into the prepared baking dish, and smooth out the top.

3. In a clean mixing bowl, whisk together the remaining cinnamon and remaining salt, the light brown sugar, rolled oats, and almond butter. Strew this mixture evenly over the batter.

4. Bake in the oven for 45 minutes until the surface of the brownies begins to crack. Allow to cool completely in the dish, before using the paper handles to lift the square out. Slice the brownie into 9 portions, and serve.

# VEGAN-STYLE PEANUT BUTTER CHEESECAKE

COOK TIME: 0 MINS | MAKES: 10-12 SERVINGS

## INGREDIENTS:

**Crust:**
- 24 vegan chocolate sandwich cookies
- 5 tbsp. almond butter, melted

**Filling:**
- 1 cup creamy peanut butter
- 2 cups vegan cream cheese
- 1 cup vegan icing sugar, sifted
- 1 1/2 cups vanilla Cocowhip

## DIRECTIONS:

1. In a high-powered food processor, pulse the sandwich cookies until you have fine crumbs. Scrape the cookie crumbs into a large mixing bowl, and drizzle with the melted almond butter. Stir with a fork until the butter is evenly incorporated into the crumbs.

2. Scrape the moistened crumbs into a large baking dish, and use the bottom of a clean glass to press them into an even base, working some of the mixture up the sides of the dish. Place in the freezer for 20 minutes.

3. Place the peanut butter and cream cheese in a large mixing bowl, and use a handheld mixer to beat for 30 seconds, until the mixture is creamy and properly incorporated. Add the icing sugar, and beat for an additional 30 seconds until you have a smooth batter. Beat the batter for a final 30-60 seconds until light and fluffy.

4. With the mixer on the lowest setting, beat in half of the vanilla Cocowhip until incorporated, then beat in the remaining half.

5. Scrape the mixture into the chilled crust, and use an offset spatula to smooth out the top. Chill the cheesecake for 5-24 hours until set.

6. When serving, wipe your knife clean between slices to ensure neat cuts and avoid a mess. Serve, and enjoy.

Printed in the USA
CPSIA information can be obtained
at www.ICGtesting.com
LVHW081036201023
761326LV00086B/94

9 781922 590350